MINI REEF YEARBOOK

ALL YOU NEED TO KNOW TO GET STARTED CORRECTLY:

Over 200 Color Photos.

A mini-reef aquarium is probably the closest an aquarist can get to the real thing. in this tank *Heliofungia*, *Xenia*, and *Porites* surround a giant clam (*Tridacna* sp.). Damselfishes and an angelfish add color to the scene. Photo by C. W. Emmens.

By Richard F. Stratton

MINI REEF

— A yearBOOK

yearBOOKS, INC.
Dr. Herbert R. Axelrod,
President
Neal Pronek
Chief Editor
Warren G. Burgess
Editor

yearBOOKS are all photo composed, color separated and designed on Scitex equipment in Neptune, N.J. with the following staff:

COMPUTER ART
Michael L. Secord
Supervisor
Sherise Buhagiar
Patti Escabi
Sandra Taylor Gale
Pat Marotta
Joanne Muzyka
Robert Onyrscuk
Tom Roberts

Advertising Sales
George Campbell
Chief
Amy Manning
Coordinator

©yearBOOKS, Inc.
1 TFH Plaza
Neptune, N.J. 07753
Completely manufactured
in Neptune, N.J.

What are yearBOOKs?

Because cultivating Mini Reef Aquariums is growing at a rapid pace, information on their selection, care and breeding is vitally needed in the marketplace. Books, the usual way information of this sort is transmitted, can be too slow. Sometimes by the time a book is written and published, the material contained therein is a year or two old...and no new material has been added during that time. Only a book in a magazine form can bring breaking stories and current information. A magazine is streamlined in production, so we have adopted certain magazine publishing techniques in the creation of this yearBOOK. Magazines also can be much cheaper than books because they are supported by advertising. To combine these assets into a great publication, we issued this yearBOOK in both magazine and book format at different prices.

Distributed in the UNITED STATES to the Pet Trade by T.F.H. Publications, Inc., One T.F.H. Plaza, Neptune City, NJ 07753; distributed in the UNITED STATES to the Bookstore and Library Trade by National Book Network, Inc. 4720 Boston Way, Lanham MD 20706; in CANADA to the Pet Trade by H & L Pet Supplies Inc., 27 Kingston Crescent, Kitchener, Ontario N2B 2T6; Rolf C. Hagen Inc., 3225 Sartelon St. Laurent-Montreal Quebec H4R 1E8; in CANADA to the Book Trade by Vanwell Publishing Ltd., 1 Northrup Crescent, St. Catharines, Ontario L2M 6P5 ; in ENGLAND by T.F.H. Publications, PO Box 15, Waterlooville PO7 6BQ; in AUSTRALIA AND THE SOUTH PACIFIC by T.F.H. (Australia), Pty. Ltd., Box 149, Brookvale 2100 N.S.W., Australia; in NEW ZEALAND by Brocklands Aquarium Ltd. 5 McGiven Drive, New Plymouth, RD1 New Zealand; in Japan by T.F.H. Publications, Japan—Jiro Tsuda, 10-12-3 Ohjidai, Sakura, Chiba 285, Japan; in SOUTH AFRICA by Lopis (Pty) Ltd., P.O. Box 39127, Booysens, 2016, Johannesburg, South Africa. Published by T.F.H. Publications, Inc.

MANUFACTURED IN THE
UNITED STATES OF AMERICA
BY T.F.H. PUBLICATIONS, INC.

CONTENTS

The multi-colored mantles of these tridacnids house algae and require lots of light. Photo by J.P. Bueles.

THE LIVING REEF AQUARIUM

Seldom has something new burst upon the scene and virtually taken everything by storm as the living reef tank. All it took was for people to get a glimpse at what they could look like. While the appeal of the typical aquarium is one primarily of beauty, the living reef tank went beyond that. True enough, a living reef tank does have beauty, and it has a unique comeliness or majesty, one that is found nowhere else—except on the incredible coral reef itself. But there is more than that. There is intrigue. There is just enough of an alien touch to it that it serves as a condiment or contrast to its stark beauty.

There is mystery, for no one is ever completely sure just what may be in their living reef display. A strange and unknown worm, for example, may emerge from wherever it had been living, swim though the tank, perhaps laying eggs, and retire, not to be seen again for years, if ever!

Certainly, one of the appeals of the living reef tank is that it more closely approximates the nature of the reef, and the interrelatedness of the animals can often be seen. As beautiful as it is, though, it doesn't really hold a candle to the reef in the wild, but it may spoil the marine hobbyist to the

An underwater reef scene in the Indo-Pacific where a lonely stand of *Acropora* is surrounded by a profusion of soft (leather) corals, probably of the genus *Dendronephthya*. Photo by Cathy Church.

extent that other marine tanks will forevermore seem sterile and artificial.

At this point, it may be worth discussing just what a living reef tank is. Misconceptions abound, so it won't hurt to clarify the point. After all, many folks seem to be under the misapprehension that any primarily invertebrate tank is a living reef tank.

Not so, and here is why: a living reef tank is one in which many of the photosynthetic animals of the reef are also kept. That means some corals, certainly, and perhaps anemones and even clams that have that capability.

Here is the situation. Coral reefs prosper in ocean environments in which the water is quite clear, and there are no upwellings of nutrients from the deep in any sizable proportions. The reefs have taken millions of years to adapt to the almost sterile waters of the tropical seas. That means that organic matter is almost completely absent. The corals and other inhabitants of the reef have developed in their tissues a multitude of zooxanthellae. These are protozoans, generally believed to be very specialized flagellates, which have photosynthetic capabilities. Although corals and other such animals feed on plankton, they are adapted for going without any food for long periods of time, and the zooxanthellae in their tissues help them accomplish just that. It is the ultimate in symbiotic

Various stony and soft corals as they appear in their natural surroundings: (1) *Pectinia* sp.; (2) *Merulina*

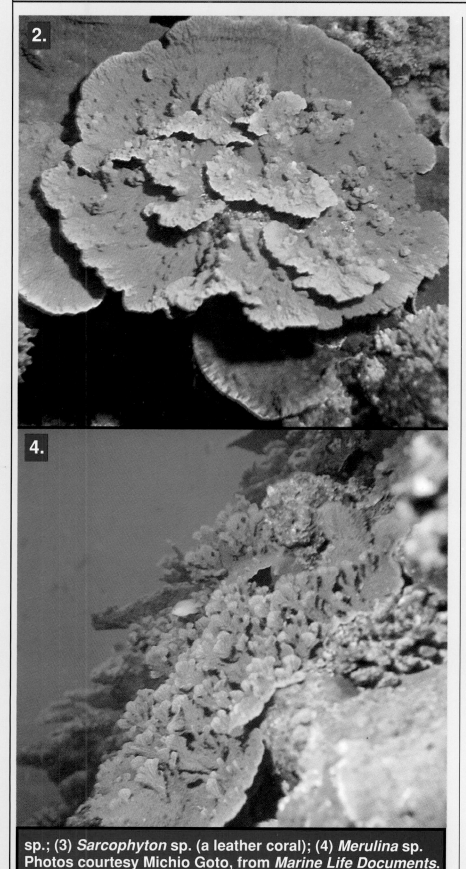

sp.; (3) *Sarcophyton* sp. (a leather coral); (4) *Merulina* sp. Photos courtesy Michio Goto, from *Marine Life Documents*.

mutualism, a situation in which two species live together for their mutual benefit. The zooxanthellae receive shelter, and they provide the host with organic compounds which they manufacture through the process of photosynthesis.

PHOTOSYNTHESIS

Since photosynthesis is such an important component of the coral reef environment, it is worth discussing in some detail here. Most people, if they are aware at all of photosynthesis, think of it in connection with plants. Even people who are not sure what it is know that plants need light in order to prosper, and some need more of it than others. Without getting into too much detail, energy to conduct the work of life is obtained through three major processes: photosynthesis, fermentation, and cellular respiration. Each of these processes is a type of energy metabolism. Photosynthesis uses light energy to synthesize a variety of food compounds. Fermentation releases energy from the reduced food compounds and is particularly important to anaerobic cells and to cells in which the oxygen supply has been depleted. Cellular respiration involves oxygen and releases a far greater amount of energy from a given amount of food than fermentation.

For there to be either fermentation or cellular respiration, on this planet at least (although it is generally believed that the first organisms on Earth were probably single-celled scavengers that inhabited tidal ponds, ingesting complex energy-rich molecules from the water and digesting them into smaller fragments), there has to be photosynthesis first. In fact, biologists often refer to the photosynthetic organisms

thermodynamically unstable. They require a continual flow of matter and energy. They need matter to build new molecules, maintain appropriate concentrations of key compounds, and replace those structures that have worn out. They need energy to assemble the molecules and to perform biological work and stem the tide of entropy.

There is little doubt that in regard to the present life on Earth, photosynthesis is the most important of the three.

There are a number of important pigments involved in photosynthesis, but the most important are the chlorophylls. These are of universal occurrence in the plant kingdom, in photosynthetic protists, and in virtually all

A reef tank that includes an alga, in this case a species of *Caulerpa*, along with the invertebrates (among others *Euphyllia divisa* and a sea pen) and fishes (*Amphiprion ocellaris* and *Centropyge heraldi*). Algae as well as other plants are primary producers. Photo by C. W. Emmens.

as the "producers," and the others are, in one way or another, "consumers." Living systems are

Matter is obtained from the environment. Energy is obtained from one of the three processes mentioned.

photosynthetic bacteria with the exception of the halobacteria. In higher plants, there are two predominant chlorophylls: chlorophyll a and chlorophyll b, which differ only slightly in structure. The chlorophylls absorb light near both ends of the visible spectrum, that is, in the blue and in the red. Were these the only chloroplast pigments

portion of the energy to chlorophyll to use in photosynthesis. Among the accessory pigments are carotenoids, such as beta carotene. The carotenoids absorb in the blue and in the blue-green and appear rich yellow in color. The phycobilins (phycocyanin

energy-absorbing "antenna" covering much of the visible spectrum. Another function of the carotenoids is to protect chlorophyll from degradation during high light intensities. Under such conditions, chlorophylls are subject to degeneration from

A mini-reef set-up with hard corals, soft corals, anemones, fishes, and algae. Note that the reef "wall" is built up against the back and one side of the tank. Photo by C. W. Emmens.

involved in photosynthesis, much of the visible spectrum would go unused. However, all photosynthetic organisms possess accessory pigments that absorb photons intermediate in energy between the red and blue and that then transfer a

and phycoerythrin), which are found in red and blue-green algae (and contribute to their colors), absorb variously in the yellow-green, yellow, and orange bands of the spectrum. Such accessory pigments, in collaboration with the chlorophylls, constitute an

oxidation, and the carotenoids help protect them during these times.

While cellular respiration involves the conversion of foods and oxygen to carbon dioxide and water, with the storage of energy, photosynthesis takes carbon dioxide and water to

Except for a few scattered animals the entire tank is covered with a coating of green algae. This is a high nitrate tank showing what animals can survive in such an environment. Certainly the green plants flourish with the nitrate content. Photo by R. Wederich.

produce food and oxygen, a process that is pushed by the energy of light. The raw materials for the photosynthetic process were known as early as 1804, but it is interesting to note that the working out of its sub-pathways had to await the end of the second world war. A very simple tool, paper partition chromatography, became available at that time. The knowledge gained from work on the atomic bomb enabled radioactive isotopes of carbon to be used to trace the fixation of carbon into carbohydrates via the use of autoradiography. These three tools (radioactive carbon, paper partition chromatography, and autoradiography) were used by scientists to investigate the metabolism of carbon dioxide supplied to photosynthesizing organisms. Thus, a true picture of the complexity of photosynthesis was attained only recently, and, like many scientific findings, it generated further questions and led to innumerable experiments (still going on today) designed to answer them. All in all, though, photosynthesis is relatively well understood today.

Although some of us consider science the greatest spectator sport of all time and will want to look into the details of photosynthesis, a complete explanation of it would take an entire book, although most such hobbyists will be content with information found in any modern college biology textbooks. Really, though, such detailed information is not needed by the hobbyist. It is sufficient to be aware that corals (and some other reef inhabitants) are photosynthetic and depend, at least in part, on that process for their nutrition.

Of course, coral polyps are able to feed on plankton, too, and newly-hatched brine shrimp will serve admirably as a substitute for that. However, there is no denying that photosynthesis is the most important source of nutrition for corals. To illustrate just how important, it should be mentioned that reef keepers often leave their displays for weeks, without having to worry about the organisms perishing of starvation! One of the reasons (besides photosynthesis) that this is possible is that the coral polyps are apparently able to absorb some nutrition from the water itself. (But an important point is that there should not be much in the way of organic life in the water. More about that later.)

THE SIMPLE APPROACH—AGAIN!

Although I will discuss, once again, a variety of gadgets for maintaining a reef tank, let us first explore a simple approach, and the beauty of this approach is that it just may be the best! Corals and

Plerogyra sinuosa, one of the bubble corals. The large vesicles, which give these corals their common name, apparently retract at night, when the tentacles are extended. Photo by M. P. & C. Piednoir.

other reef animals positively thrive, prosper, and even reproduce in this (relatively) simple system. (To be honest, they do so in other systems, too, but the most successful ones I have seen have been in this one.)

The most essential equipment here consists of a good protein skimmer, some power heads for water movement, and good wide-spectrum lighting. First, let's deal with the protein skimmer.

It should be pointed out that this is one device that has gained adherents, rather than lost them. And more and more reef keepers are turning to it as the main device for maintaining the water quality in the tank. Remember, a protein skimmer is more properly called a "water fractionater" (although hardly anyone calls it that!), and it works because of the tendency of organic compounds to adhere to the surface of the water area. Without getting into the hydrophilic (water attracting) and hydrophobic (water repulsing) aspects of organic molecules, foaming in the water tends to "gather up" organic molecules and carry them with it. Thus, if we place a collector, such as the "cup" which is used so often with protein skimmers, we get rid of troublesome organics before they have a chance to break down. Remember, the water of the coral reef is so bereft of organic matter that it could nearly be called sterile. That is the type of water that our coral reef organisms have adapted to, and the invertebrates are the least tolerant of change. For that reason, it should not

Euphyllia glabrescens have tentacles shaped like narrow fingers but with slightly inflated tips. The polyp tentacles are unable to completely retract and so are always extended during the day. The alga is *Caulerpa taxifolia*. Photo by M. P. & C. Piednoir.

Euphyllia glabrescens. Some of the tentacles are extremely elongate, but the reason is not known. Could this have something to do with spawning or defense? Photo by M. P. & C. Piednoir.

be surprising that a device that gets rid of organics before they even get a chance to break down has found such favor.

Basically, you have two choices when contemplating a protein skimmer: the air-driven types and the venturi skimmers. The air-driven types need a powerful air pump, and the bubbles should be checked nearly twice a day. It will take experience to get just the right flow, the one that is most productive for your tank. Most reef keepers are ambivalent about foam in the collection cup. If it is there, it demonstrates that the protein skimmer is working properly, but it is also an indication that there are organic waste molecules in the tank. Perhaps too much? If there is no foam present, the hobbyist worries about the proper functioning of the protein skimmer, when the simple truth may be that good aquarium practices simply have the water in such good shape that the protein skimmer has nothing to pick up.

If the redox potential (to be discussed later) is sufficiently high, the hobbyist has nothing to worry about if there is no foam in the cup. But don't get overconfident. Check the cup daily, and, of course, it should be emptied daily (if there is anything in it).

Even within the air-driven types there are differences. Some fit inside the tank. It is the opinion of most hobbyists, after many years of experience,

***Euphyllia cristata*.
Corals, through
their feeding, act as
part of the filtration
of a well set-up
mini-reef aquarium.
Photo by M. P. & C.
Piednoir.**

of bubbles, you have to be sure that the water level is just right.) Most hobbyists seem to prefer the counter-current air-driven protein skimmers. This means that the water usually comes in from the top and moves downward in the opposite direction of the bubbles.

A primary drawback of the air-driven types is that they need constant attention in regard to the flow and type of bubbles. Small bubbles are best. They are not so buoyant and enable the bubbles to stay in contact with the water long enough for the surface contact reaction to take place. Large bubbles are too buoyant and rise too quickly, not allowing sufficient time for the aforementioned reaction. Sadly, it is even possible to have the bubbles too small. If they rise too slowly they may dissipate in the water, releasing the proteins and organics into the water once again. Since valves tend to slip and even the special airstones for the protein skimmer become clogged, the bubble flow has a tendency to change, so the flow must be checked at least daily. A good strong air pump is needed, and the airstones will have to be replaced promptly when you can no longer get them to produce small bubbles. The airstones tend to become clogged even more quickly in ocean water than they do in fresh water.

Because of the problems mentioned above, the hobbyist may wish to consider the venturi protein

that these are difficult to get of sufficient height, and they are easy to forget about when they actually require even more attention than the outside types. (Besides emptying the collection cup and maintaining a proper flow skimmer. The main drawback to these devices is that they are more expensive. However, they don't require an air pump or airstones. They receive their name from the fact that the venturi principle is utilized in producing the bubbles. These skimmers

skimmers require much less adjusting on the part of the reef keeper than do the air-driven skimmers. Nevertheless, they should be checked frequently for foam in the cup and to make sure that the bubble flow is correct.

Whichever type you get, a

Nearly all experienced reef keepers like to get protein skimmers that are rated for twice the size of the tank that they are actually going to utilize. The point is that you can't overdo it, and a protein skimmer that is not adequate for your tank is basically useless. Besides,

A well functioning mini-reef tank. Among the corals growing luxuriantly are *Goniopora pendulus* and *Euphyllia diversa*; the fishes include clown anemonefishes, a flame angelfish and a small yellow acanthurid. Photo by C. W. Emmens.

utilize a venturi valve that, as water passes through it, sucks air that mixes with incoming water. This air and water mixture is then injected by the venturi valve, under considerable force, into the skimmer body. Once they are set at the proper air and water mixture, venturi-driven

really important point is to get a relatively high skimmer. After all, the higher the skimmer, the longer the bubbles stay in contact with the water; hence the advantage of the higher skimmers. Protein skimmers are rated according to the size tank that they can service.

manufacturers rate their products on the average of what a reef keeper is going to stock in his tank, and advanced reef keepers can really load the tank to the brim with various corals and invertebrates.

Certainly, if you are going to rely primarily on the protein skimmer, you don't want to skimp because of price. That approach can truly be "pound wise and penny foolish." The point is that you could lose priceless specimens from having

An important point here is that the height and rated tank capacity of the protein skimmer is more important than whether it is air-driven or venturi-driven. Even though air-driven

type you use, you should have an intake that skims the water from the surface, as that is where the organics tend to congregate, and you should have a good prefilter that is

The mixture of fishes and invertebrates must be carefully considered. Many fishes treat the invertebrates as food rather than tank mates. Some aquarists do without fishes altogether in their reef tanks. Photo by C. W. Emmens.

skimped on the protein skimmer. A large skimmer will save you money over the long run and will benefit the health and well-being of your specimens. Another benefit of the extra large skimmer is that it will increase the redox potential of your tank. That is, it will increase its ability to bounce back from organic contaminants.

skimmers require more tinkering and tweaking, some reef keepers feel that they are superior because they produce a more productive foam. Obviously, this is open to debate, and you will find adherents of both types of skimmers among reef hobbyists.

In any case, whichever

easy to clean. That is, you should have easy access to it, for it should be cleaned at least weekly, and twice a week would be better. The point is that it should be visible and accessible. When something is out of sight and difficult to access, the natural propensity would be not to clean it frequently, and that would be disastrous! Also, the barrel of your protein skimmer should be cleaned at least every three months. You don't want a build-up of organics there either, and it is important to be able to clearly see what is going on in the column of your skimmer device.

COMPLICATIONS: FILTERING DEVICES

There are two main take care of the former all by itself...in my opinion. Other reef keepers will be horrified by such a remark. These are the technophiles (of which I am one, too, actually), and there is just no way that they could be satisfied with a mere protein skimmer with a pre-filter that is serviced regularly. That is too simple. Besides, it just and fluidized biological filters. True technophiles will probably have both!

TRICKLE FILTERS

Trickle filtration was probably first adopted by the reef keepers. Certainly, it can be used successfully with a reef tank. These filters are efficient at breaking down organic compounds from ammonia

It is impossible to accurately determine how many and what species will thrive from the "living rocks" that are placed in a reef tank. Of course the aquarist can add selected animals (like the giant clam) once the tank has become established and is running well. Photo by C. W. Emmens.

requirements for a living reef tank: super clean water and sun-like lighting. A good protein skimmer that is properly maintained, coupled with good aquarium practices, can makes sense to them to have insurance. They would insist on having some biological filtration. There are two excellent candidates to fulfill such a requirement: trickle filters to nitrite to nitrates. The great hunt in the trickle filtration industry has been to develop the wet part of the filter for anaerobic bacteria to break down the nitrates. This has been the difficult part of the problem. As far as I know, a successful nitrate component to the filter has not been developed. Everything has to be done just right, or you can get toxic releases from the anaerobic bacteria that can most certainly kill some or all of the marine life in your tank. It only takes one or two such failures to discourage efforts in this direction.

FLUIDIZED BIOLOGICAL FILTRATION

This device is a good candidate for the reef tank. In fact, I have seen setups with a prefilter, a trickle filter, and a fluidized filter all in a line. If you are going to put the protein skimmer into such a system, it should be placed before any of the other devices.

The fluidized filter has

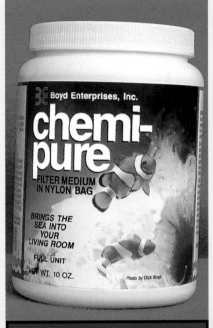

Products are available that remove ammonia and other nitrogenous waste products harmful to fishes and other animals. Photo courtesy Boyd Enterprises.

much to recommend it (as does the trickle filter, for that matter). The basic idea is to introduce clean water to the filter. Its only function is a biological one, so no particulate matter should be introduced into the filter. As a matter of fact, this is a good rule for all biological filters: keep the particulate matter separate from them. That is why the reverse-flow undergravel filter is such an improvement over the regular undergravel filter.

In any case, the idea is to keep the sand in suspension so that it is surrounded by water, and the bacteria that reside upon each granule can have access to the nutrients in the water and can process it with dispatch. The efficiency of the fluidized filter is amazing, and, in theory, it should never need cleaning and it should require very little in the way of maintenance—perhaps an occasional replacement of a power head, as they, of course, don't last forever. The only drawback to the device is that it has the same limitations as the undergravel filter and the trickle filter in that it will not metabolize the nitrates that are the end product of all their work. Nitrates are much less toxic than ammonia or nitrites, of course, but it would be nice to be rid of them, too. However, if you are utilizing a good protein skimmer, that should greatly reduce the metabolites to be processed so that the nitrate level should be low,

Ozone generators are widely available and can be effective as destroyers of bacteria if common-sense precautions are taken during their use. Photo courtesy of Ultralife Reef Products.

and water changes can be that much more infrequent.

Although I am an ardent advocate of regular and frequent partial water changes, the ultimate goal of the reef keeper and other marine hobbyists is to make such changes unnecessary.

LIVE ROCK

Live rocks are rocks that have been in tropical seas and transported for use in the hobbyists' tanks. In fact, many live rocks are being cultured now, much like pearls. Part of the reason is the convenience of doing so, and part of it is that environmental groups were taking a jaundiced look at the practice of removing rocks from the ocean.

The idea behind live rocks is that marine life grows upon these rocks that not only can be of interest in the aquarium, but some of it can actually help maintain water quality. For example, it is believed that there are anaerobic bacteria deep within the rocks that help process nitrates and reduce their level. Also, there are countless worms and other invertebrates that live within the rock and help make the aquarium a more complete representation of the fabulous ocean in your home or office.

One of the ironies of live rock is that the usual practice has been to "cure" it by keeping it in the dark for several weeks, changing the water frequently. This leaves very little alive in the rocks. I like the approach

This double bubble aquarium was manufactured and designed by Aampro of Las Vegas, Nevada. It is about 125 x 60 x 250 cm (48 x 22 x 96 inches) and comes complete with all the necessary filters, aerators, etc.

of placing the rock immediately into the aquarium. No other life should be in the tank, of course, and you may experience a little odor from the tank as some of the organisms die off, but keep the protein skimmer going (and service it daily!), make frequent partial water changes, and some of the organisms will survive and begin to flourish. Live rock will be the foundation for your living reef tank. The corals and other invertebrates will be added after the living rock has

stabilized and has begun to thrive. It is important at this point to make sure that you haven't included a mantis shrimp or bristle worms at this stage of the game. A baited trap can help ascertain whether you have any such animals. The time to get rid of them is now.

LIGHTING

One of the problems in providing proper lighting is that the captured (or cultivated) organisms have adapted to light at different depths. And the light the

A small piece of living rock may contain dozens of species of coelenterates, sponges, and worms, plus a few crustaceans, molluscs, and even a sea squirt or two. Sponges may also encrust the surface and cracks of the rock. Many of these animals survive in the aquarium and eventually produce rich growths that not only look good but help condition the water. Art by John R. Quinn.

reef receives is incredible. It has been measured at ten feet at noon at 100,000 lux (one lux is the amount of light produced by one candle at a distance of one meter). Remember that the way the corals have adapted to such an environment is by a symbiotic relationship with the zooxanthellae in their tissues. The corals give off carbon dioxide and ammonia as waste products, and the zooxanthellae utilize them in the process of photosynthesis, which results in nutrients that it shares with its host. Now, the problem is how much light and at what spectrum do we need to make all of this possible in our tanks?

Fortunately, it is not always noon in the tropics, and the corals are not all at ten feet (thirty foot depths are about the average). That means that we don't have to worry about supplying lights that create 100,000 lux. But we do need to have lighting of reasonably high intensity, and we need to be sure that it illuminates in certain essential areas of the lighting spectrum. The light producing bulbs or tubes should have a minimum of red and orange light, as this light is filtered out quickly in the water. That means that not many organisms are adapted to this light and thus depend on it, but you do need a minimum amount, just to be safe, and it also helps improve the appearance of the aquarium. In addition, these lights should produce a small amount of ultraviolet (UV) light. This light is between 320 to 400 nanometers (nm). This is not the extremely hazardous UV-B or UV-C ultraviolet light that is used in ultraviolet sterilizers, but it can cause a sunburn. (After all, we are trying to sunburn and eventually a tan.

Although corals are exposed to considerable ultraviolet light in the tropics, they have natural filtering compounds to help protect them from it, so we are not certain just how much of it is essential for presence of ultraviolet light also causes bioflorescence in the corals. That is, some corals will literally glow when this type of light is present. When it is missing, they may still be colorful but will lack the iridescence that the ultraviolet light produces.

Proper lighting is extremely important for the animals in a reef tank. Among others the corals, for example these *Anthelia* and *Acropora*, harbor zooxanthellae in their tissues, which need bright light to carry on their photosynthetic processes. Photo by C. W. Emmens.

duplicate natural sunlight as closely as possible in the most cost-effective way.) In fact, if you were to lie in a bathing suit under the aquarium lamp close enough and long enough you could develop a their well-being. Nevertheless, ultraviolet light helps improve the appearance of the corals, and its presence helps produce the vivid colors typical of reef invertebrates. The fact is that the To try to replicate the light intensity impinging on the reef, many hobbyists are using metal halide lights with a high Kelvin number (greater than 5500 K). In addition, they augment this light with blue light from specially-designed tubes. By using both types of lighting, the reef keepers are able to not only provide light that is visually appealing to the viewer, but also light capable of providing enough energy to drive the metabolic processes of the zooxan-thellae within the inverte-brates.

There are different approaches to obtaining the wide spectrum and the light intensity that is needed for the corals and other photo-synthetic organisms. The fascinating thing is that it is now possible. It was not long ago that the only way anyone could keep coral or tropical anemones was by having them in an area that received direct sunlight. And remember, even sunlight at high noon in temperate areas is not equivalent to the natural light in the tropics. Still, some diehards managed to keep corals and such

things by the skillful use of skylights and even sunlight collectors. But that was the hard way. Now it can be done with artificial lighting. But it gets a little

Different animals prefer different light levels and should be placed at the depth in a tank that best suits them. The most light-loving should be near the surface, those that require less intensity at deeper levels. Photo by B. Degen.

complex. Let's take a quick look at exactly what is needed, what some of the problems are in filling the needs, and what some of the solutions have been.

First, the intensity could be easily taken care of with metal halide lighting, but this type of lighting produces quite a bit of heat,

and the lighting has to either be kept high up off the cover of the tank, or fans must be employed to clear out the hot air from underneath the hood. Second, corals need actinic light. That means light that causes a reaction and usually refers to light that is "spiked" in the blue part of the spectrum. There are good fluorescent tubes that supply this. One of the things to get used to is that with a reef tank, lighting is one of the most important components. For that reason, there are not merely one or two fluorescent bulbs in the hood. There may be six or eight of different types—and these may be supplemented by hanging metal halide lights!

Fortunately, light bulb manufacturers have responded to the needs of the aquarium trade, and specific bulbs are made even for reef tanks. It is possible to have either metal arc or metal halide bulbs. These can be supplemented with special actinic bulbs for the blue light requirements. This combination looks more natural than an all-fluorescent set up, and has a good effect on tank residents, too.

WATER FLOW: CURRENTS AND TIDAL ACTION

All the animals of the coral reef are adapted to currents. That is because need clean water; we already know that. They also cannot take any sediment whatsoever. The currents help keep any sediment, wherever it may have come from, washed off the corals (and anemones). This works in the reef tank, too. And, although there is not normally much in the way of tidal action in the the configuration of the reef itself. That is, the current can flow through tunnel-like areas and be diverted or bounced back into other areas, much like tidal action. Finally, it must be admitted that tidal action influences the currents even on patch reefs, and on outer reefs, too, for that matter. In the ocean

Water flow is another important factor when setting up a reef tank. Some animals prefer still water while others require a current to be at their best. The aquarist must find out the needs of his or her charges before designing the tank. Photo by J. Manzione.

corals only grow in areas in which currents flow. And that is because the currents bring them plankton. But there is another reason. Corals reefs, there is often a back and forth surge, which amounts to the same thing. This back and forth flow is caused by a change in the direction of currents and by everything is interconnected, so the flow of the tides is mirrored to some degree even far out to sea.

In any case, a back and

Power filters are commonly used for mini-reef aquaria. There are a number of different types to choose from. Photo courtesy of Hagen.

carrying away waste material. Another factor for consideration is that a good strong current probably stimulates the feeding response.

Obviously, too strong a current will be counterproductive, as it will only cause the corals to withdraw their polyps, as they would do during a tropical storm. What we want is a current that flows past and around the corals. This can be accomplished by strategically placed power heads. One of the most popular configurations is to have one or two at each end of the tank and have them controlled by a timer that alternates their use. in that way you get the back and forth tidal motion I have talked about so much. One of the important

benefits of this action is that any debris is kept in suspension so that it can easily be picked up by the out-takes for your protein skimmer (and biological filters, if you have them).

REEF MENTALITY

Obviously, the reef aquarium is not for everyone. You certainly have to be something of a technophile for the pursuit of this hobby. You also have to be a *bona fide* student of the ocean and its inhabitants—and that includes the invertebrates. Everyone knows about killer whales and sharks, but how many people know about the invertebrates and, yes, even the bacteria, that in many ways make life possible for all the "higher" organisms?

To many people, the

forth flow is what most hobbyists prefer in their tanks. They feel that it somehow keeps the corals and other invertebrates more healthy in appearance. Part of the reason for this is probably that it does keep them clean and free of any debris, although, certainly, there should be very little debris in a reef tank. Just the action of the water no doubt has a beneficial effect, too, as it stimulates the corals and anemones. That is, it makes them more active. This may be partly due to the more natural environment, but it is doubtless in part due to the fact that the water is bringing in a continual supply of oxygen and is

Artificial sea salts are widely available in a number of different formulations. Photo courtesy of Coralife/ Energy Savers.

The tentacles of the free-living *Heliofungia actiniformis* are always extended during the day. They are usually gray, blue or green in color with a light-colored tip. Photo by Dr. H. R. Axelrod.

living reef tank is absolutely the ultimate in aquarium keeping. It combines beauty, rarity of inhabitants, and infers that the reef keeper must be a person of uncommon knowledge in order to accomplish the feat of maintaining such a wonderful tank. All of that is true, sort of. Certainly, the reef tank is the ultimate status tank now, which means that people who

have not really learned all that much about them but have money are willing to pay to have them set up and maintained. That would seem to impeach the last part of the assumptions automatically assumed, but it doesn't really. At least, I don't know of any wealthy people who have ignored their tanks, even when they are maintained professionally. They simply can't resist

learning about them, and, more often than not, begin to take over more and more of their maintenance.

There is a price to be paid for such exalted status. Now, suddenly, the fishes are secondary. The invertebrates come first. Most reef keepers defer adding any fishes until all the invertebrates are prospering. Some of them never do get around to adding them. They have

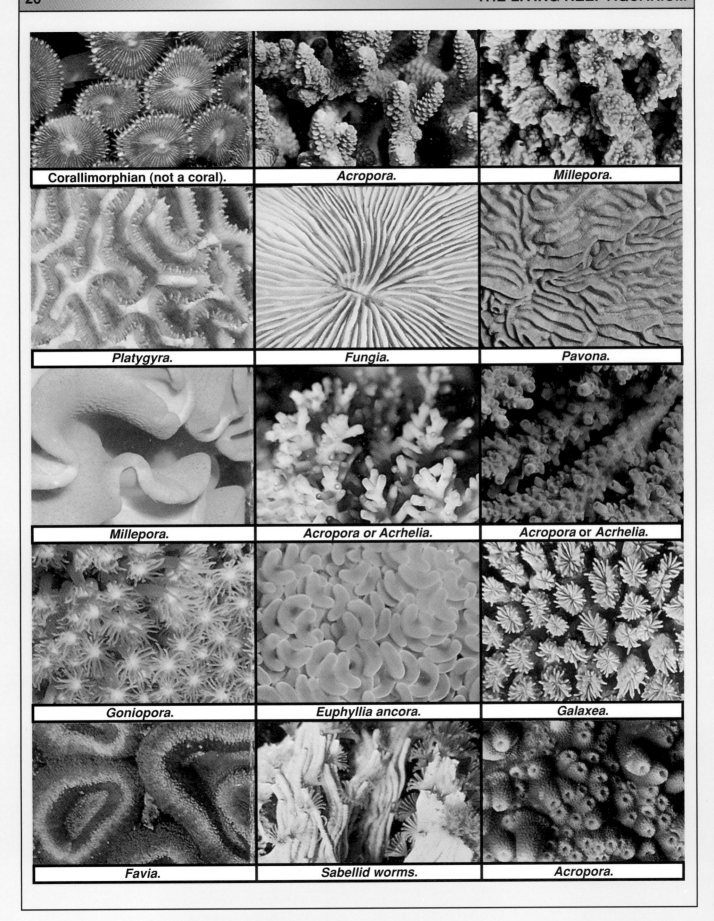

Corallimorphian (not a coral). | *Acropora.* | *Millepora.*

Platygyra. | *Fungia.* | *Pavona.*

Millepora. | *Acropora* or *Acrhelia.* | *Acropora* or *Acrhelia.*

Goniopora. | *Euphyllia ancora.* | *Galaxea.*

Favia. | *Sabellid worms.* | *Acropora.*

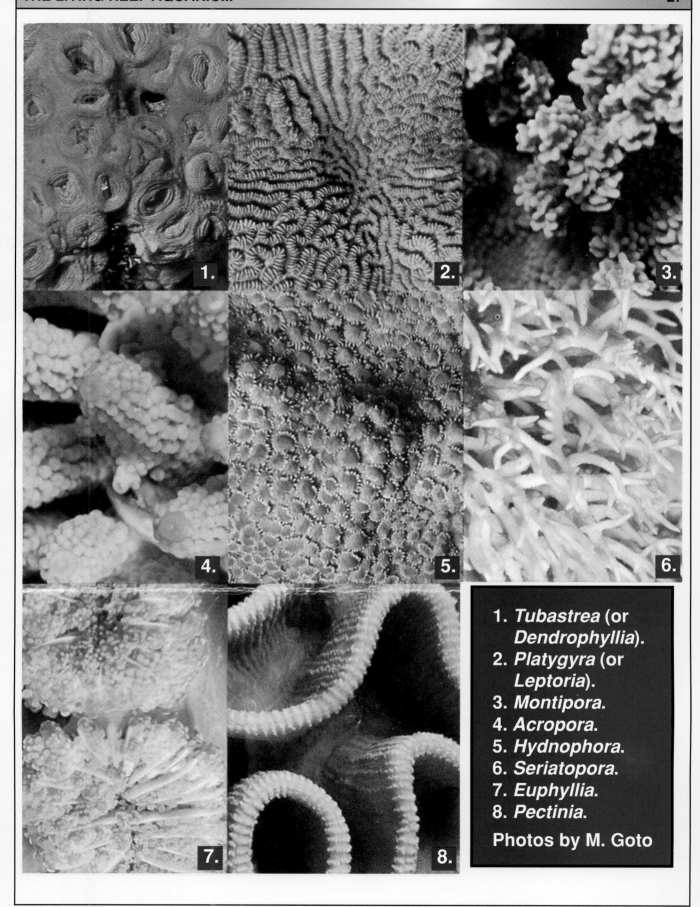

1. *Tubastrea* (or *Dendrophyllia*).
2. *Platygyra* (or *Leptoria*).
3. *Montipora*.
4. *Acropora*.
5. *Hydnophora*.
6. *Seriatopora*.
7. *Euphyllia*.
8. *Pectinia*.

Photos by M. Goto

By using the currents in the aquarium to your advantage, you can help circulate food, especially the variety of liquid invertebrate foods now available in pet shops. Photo courtesy of Coralife/Energy Savers.

become so attached to their reef tank that they don't want to take a chance with any fishes. Still, fishes are an important part of reef life. Even so, the fish population should be kept low, as their more active metabolism will put a strain on your requirement of super quality water if you place too many fishes in the tank.

Reef keepers are not mere status seekers. Even if they start out that way, they become true students of the ocean, and the more they do so, the more their tanks become truly a bit of the fabulous sea. More than any other hobbyists, as a group, they are aware of the interrelatedness of life, and of our ties to the resplendent ocean.

INVERTEBRATES FOR THE REEF TANK

Some of the invertebrates will come with the live rocks that will normally be the first thing that you place in a reef tank. Not only are live rocks a component of the inhabitants of the reef, but they also provide some filtration in that they are believed to contain, deep within their innards, anaerobic bacteria that break down nitrates. When we finally get sufficient action of that type, the breaking down of the nitrates, we will finally achieve the ultimate goal of marine aquarists: to eliminate the need for water changes. That day may never come, but it is always something to strive toward. And even if the goal is never met, we have already come a long way, in that a system can be so good that, along with good practices by the hobbyist, water changes can be kept to a bare minimum. It is mainly a philosophical ideal at this time, as water changes are not really troublesome or expensive in these days of excellent marine salts.

In any case, it is a thin line of demarcation to decide which organisms should be listed as inhabitants of the system

Opened soft corals photographed at 40 feet at Opal Reef, Great Barrier Reef, Australia, by Dr. G. R. Allen.

and which should be listed with the filtering equipment, for many of the invertebrates, including many of the coral polyps and even some of the anemones, could be listed as "filtering agents" too, for they do process the water themselves. So, realizing that the listing is to some degree artificial, I will proceed to recommend some invertebrates for the reef tank. Not all of these will be solid recommend-ations, but I will list the cautionary aspects of the organisms along with the benefits they bring to a reef system.

It is worth mentioning here that the demand for live rock has become sufficient that it is being cultivated in the ocean by several enterprises, and it is being offered in different categories. For example, it is possible to order live rock that has coral budding on it and is generally guaranteed to be free of

bristleworms and mantis shrimp, the two main nightmares of the reef keeper. Even cultivated live rock such as that may have unknown worms and other species deep within,

One of the favorites of marine aquarists is the bright golden *Tubastrea aurea*. The polyps, however, are generally retracted during the day and expanded at night.

for the method of cultivation is to place the rock in protected areas in the tropical ocean. (At the time of this writing, most of this is being done in southern Florida.) In any case, the situation for

obtaining live rock has never been better than it is right now.

Everyone wants to keep stony corals, as they are what build the coral reefs, reef patches, and atolls, but most species are a challenge, as water conditions have to be just right. And many species seem to require strong currents, consisting of surges that are difficult to duplicate in the home aquarium. Nevertheless, I plan to list some stony corals, and I will start with them, rather than go in phylogenetic order with reef species. That is, I will begin with stony corals, starting with the most robust and easily kept species, and progress to other photosynthetic organisms for the reef tank. Finally, I will list non-photosynthetic organisms which might do well in a reef tank and would add to its appeal.

CORALS: CLASS ANTHOZOA
Corals are members of the superclass Cnidaria,

which consists of three classes: Hydrozoa (hydras, fire corals, and the Portuguese Man-O-War), Scyphozoa (jellyfish), and Anthozoa (soft corals, stony corals, and anemones). All three classes, often referred to as coelenterates, are simple animals with one

direct opening to the gut. All have stinging cells in their tentacles, but those in the corals and most of the anemones are unable to hurt the skin of the human hand unless the person has extremely sensitive skin or is extremely allergic to them.

Although the hydras, jellyfishes, and corals are separate classes, they often appear quite similar in many ways. In fact, the anemone is sometimes referred to as an upside-down jellyfish. Also, some of the corals that we refer to as such are, technically, anemones! Although we tend to think of corals and anemones as practically plants (after all, they are pretty much stationary, and

they even "perform" photosynthesis), they are animals and will prove it by even attacking each other, albeit in slow motion. The threat is serious enough that the reef keeper must leave a little space between different species, as one colony could be "wiped out" by the chemical warfare of another. And many anemones are not suitable for a true reef aquarium because of their ability to move about and thus pose a danger to the corals. In spite of all these considerations, it is

possible to position your corals and anemones so that they truly look like a miniature reef.

Bubble Coral (*Plerogyra sinuosa*)

The common name of this species is a very appropriate description, as the polyps of the coral are protected by day by a mass of bubbles. The bubbles are often snow-white in coloration, but they can be pink to fawn also. At night the bubbles deflate, and the coral erects long, flowing

One of the soft corals of the genus *Dendronephthya* from Oman. The combination of white stalks with the golden polyps is very attractive. Photo by T. Woodward.

tentacles to feed upon the plankton and even small shrimp. This is a hardy species, partly because it is easily fed, even taking bits of clam. Many coral species have polyps that are so small that they must be fed a special liquid food which contains particles small enough for them to "capture." However, many of the coral species that do well in captivity will take newly-hatched brine shrimp, which this species also will take, and which should be fed after the lights are turned out. Once a week is often enough for feeding, as this species also receives nutrients from photosynthesis. The fact is that they rarely need feeding if they receive the proper lighting.

Bubble corals come from throughout the Indo-Pacific, and they vary slightly in color. They are hardy and a good species for the beginning reef tanker who insists on trying stony corals. They will prosper and grow at a remarkable rate when the tank conditions are kept up to par for them.

Tooth Coral (*Euphyllia picteti*)

This is another species that is a favorite and is quite hardy in the aquarium. It is quite green in color because of the type and amount of zooxanthellae in its tissues, and it will need good

Only the skeleton of the organ-pipe coral, *Tubipora musica*, was used in marine aquaria as a decoration mainly because of its red coloration. Photo by Dr. H. R. Axelrod.

lighting in order to prosper. This is one of the types of corals that will show a fluorescent color under proper lighting. Again, this species is capable of taking large pieces of food, but, once again, you can keep feeding at a minimum with

good lighting. Keeping feeding to a minimum is a desirable goal because of the need for super-clean water. This species hails from the Indian Ocean, where it exhibits some geographical variation in coloration, with some specimens showing more of a blue coloration, while others are fluorescent green with orange tips.

Frogspawn Coral (*Euphyllia divisa*)

The somewhat ribald name for this species of *Euphyllia*, a popular genus of corals for the reef tank, comes from the large tentacles, which are generally round, transparent white, and vaguely resemble the spawn of certain group spawning frogs. This species thrives on good lighting and weekly feedings of newly-hatched brine shrimp. The brine shrimp should be placed in the tank at night with the tank in total darkness. It is a good idea to turn off the filters at this time so that the brine shrimp are not immediately filtered out. Keep the power heads going, though, and provide plenty of aeration.

Dogtooth Coral (*Euphyllia fimbriata*)

Actually, the entire genus *Euphyllia* is variously called "dogtooth" and "vase" corals. They are them, including this species, prosper in good lighting and perhaps one feeding a week of newly-hatched brine shrimp. This species varies in coloration from beige to bright green. As with the other species of this genus, they should be given good lighting and fed not more often than once a week.

Large ones are often damaged in transport, and it cannot be emphasized too strongly that half the secret of successfully keeping live corals is to get specimens that are in good shape to begin with. Those that have been broken off or damaged may develop a fungus or bacterial infection. There are many species of brain coral, including

Sarcophyton trocheliophorum, one of the more attractive leather corals, is reported to reach a diameter of more than a meter in nature. In an aquarium they can double their size in a year with proper lighting and diet. Photo by M. P. & C. Piednoir.

quite popular with reef tankers, because they are relatively hardy for stony corals, and they are attractive. Nearly all of

Brain Coral (*Diploria strigosa*)

This species hails from the Caribbean, and small specimens make excellent inhabitants for the reef tank.

completely different genera from the Pacific and Indian Oceans, and while not all of them are as good candidates for the reef tank as this one is, they are generally of a striking appearance in the home reef tank. They like good lighting and the less-than-weekly feeding of newly-hatched live brine shrimp, alternating with the specially formulated "plankton."

Although all corals are aggressive toward rival colonies, many brain corals are particularly problematic in this way, with their specialized long stinging polyps for defending the perimeters from other corals. So the prudent reef keeper will make certain that there is an extra buffer space around the brain corals. Brain corals, in particular, do well in tanks that have power heads that provide an artificial tidal surge.

Moon Coral (*Favites* species)

Moon corals are closely related to the brain corals and resemble them, but the ridges, or meanders, are divided into numerous single units, each housing a polyp. The polyps are inter-linked, which can be a problem with this type of coral, for collectors cannot simply hack off a piece of one of these corals

and expect them to thrive in an aquarium. These species come from all over the tropical seas, and they need a steady source of medium lighting. That is, they should be placed down

This species of leather coral, *Alcyonium brioniense*, may become imported on living rock. It has symbiotic algae and therefore needs plenty of light. But it does accept all kinds of artificial plankton if it is small enough. Photo by G. Marcuse.

low in the tank, but they should not be placed in a shaded area. Moon corals

are among the many corals that show a striking fluorescence under ultraviolet light.

Sun Coral (*Tubastrea aurea*)

Here is a coral that should have shade, rather than extreme light. In the wild these specimens live in caves or in deep water, so specimens will need to be shielded from the intense lighting provided for the other corals and anemones. They are worth keeping because they provide contrast to your other invertebrates. They receive their common name from the bright orange coloration that most of them exhibit. Since they have no symbiotic algae, they need regular feedings, and this is the drawback to keeping this species in the reef tank. Some hobbyists feed each polyp separately with a small syringe. Such dedication is not possessed by all reef tankers equally, but well-fed colonies will increase in size by producing new polyps near the mature ones.

Organ Pipe Coral (*Tubipora musica*)

Back in the bad old days of dead coral skeletons in

the marine aquarium, this was a popular species because of its unusual shape and red coloration. Unfortunately, it is not easily kept alive in the reef aquarium (keeping in mind that all stony corals are something of a challenge). After success with the more hardy species of stony corals, you may want to take on the challenge of keeping this "old friend," which was well known but only as the remains of a dead creature.

Plate Coral (*Heliofungia actiniformis*)

As will be seen later, many species of anemones are confused with corals. This is a coral that is occasionally confused with an anemone, as it has the appearance of many of the anemone species. While most corals are composed of a colony of polyps, *Heliofungia* is a solitary polyp with one central mouth. Zooxanthellae can tint them green or pink. As well as deriving nourishment from the zooxanthellae, *Heliofungia* will take newly-hatched brine shrimp and even chopped fish in small quantities.

Soft Corals: Order Alcyonacea

These are actually the corals that are most found in reef aquaria, as they are considerably more hardy and less demanding than all but the hardiest of the stony corals. With many of these, however, there will be a problem of attachment, since you can't just place them in an aquarium as is the case with the heavy stony corals.

A yellow sponge, *Axinella damicornis*, is growing on a firm substrate (probably covered with a red alga). A zoanthid, *Parazoanthus axinellae*, is growing on the sponge. Photo by G. Marcuse.

Most need strong wide-spectrum lighting and the same super-quality water that is necessary for the stony corals. Feeding is also very similar with these corals. A once-a-week feeding of newly-hatched brine shrimp will suffice. As is the case with the stony corals, most of the species feed at night.

Red Cauliflower Coral (*Dendronephthya rubeola*)

This is one of the most attractive of the soft corals, and it adds to its charms by being one of the easier specimens to maintain. It lives on sand and mud sediments in the Indo-Pacific regions, where it anchors itself into position with a number of thick and fleshy root-like growths from its base. The method of attachment makes the species easier to collect than those that grow from rock and have to be damaged to some degree to be removed from the anchoring rock. During the day, these species contract into a red and white ball. The loose calcareous spicules that support the flesh project through the outer layer and can harm the ungloved hand of the hobbyist. Under subdued lighting or at night, the animal takes in water to feed. The species should be fed liquid foods and nothing larger than newly-hatched live brine shrimp (which may, in fact, be too large for many specimens).

Pulse Coral (*Anthelia glauca*)

These Indonesian imports are justifiably becoming more popular. They are easy to keep, and they can be expected to spread and multiply in the aquarium. The pulse coral consists of a coral to a rocky substrate. The common name for the species comes from the continual rhythmic opening and closing of the polyps as they feed. The species needs good lighting, a good current of water, and feeding at least be expected to increase in size. The species are normally sold already attached to a small rock. The desirable specimens have an undamaged base with no decomposing areas. Leather coral should be fed liquid food

A selection of coral skeletons. This is becoming a thing of the past as aquarists are more and more excited about being able to keep the living corals in their tanks. Photo by Dr. H. R. Axelrod.

cluster of very feathery polyps that are joined at the base to form a foot anchoring the

Any substrate that can be used on a reef (or in a reef tank) is eventually used. Animals even grow in or on one another. For example the bulge near the base of this coral probably houses a gall crab. Photo by Dr. H. R. Axelrod.

once a week of liquid foods and newly-hatched brine shrimp.

Leather Coral (*Sarcophyton trocheliphorum*)

This is the most commonly imported of the leather corals that are widespread throughout the tropical Indo-Pacific region. The common name comes from the texture and color of the animal when the polyps are retracted. Given good lighting this species does very well and can

about three times a week, and a special effort should be made to keep the top of the coral clean. If the natural currents in the tank doesn't do the job, utilize air tubing to siphon debris.

SEA FANS AND GORGONIANS (ORDER: *GORGONACEAE*)

Sea Fan (*Gorgonia flabellum*)

Once again, this is a species that was once best known as a dead skeleton used to decorate home aquaria after

A lace bryozoan may hitch-hike into your aquarium on living rock. These very interesting animals often assume some bizarre shapes as seen here. Photo by Dr. H. R. Axelrod.

being treated with a non-toxic coating. They looked like black lace. In life, they are even more beautiful, usually having a purplish hue. Once again, one of the secrets to success

species that does best with an undulating current (tidal effect). It will reward you for your efforts at providing that, as a sea fan looks beautiful swaying back and forth with

rule is that the thick-fingered species are generally more robust and easier to maintain than those species with very thin branches. Species are sold already attached to a

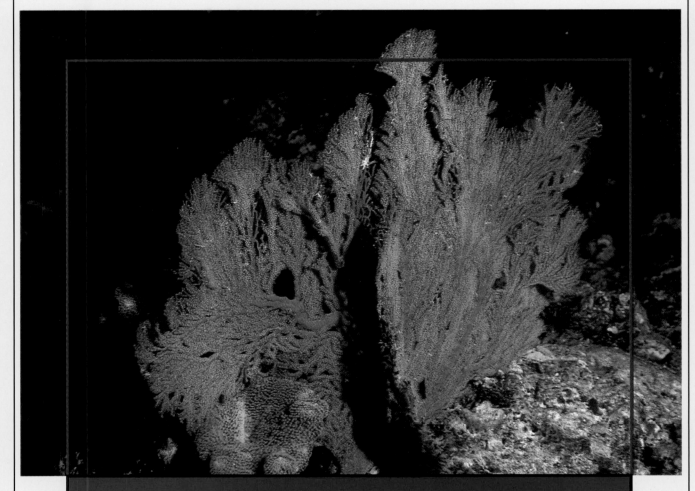

This gorgonian, or sea fan, *Acabaria*, is quite colorful. Be very sure that the base is intact and does not have any decaying animals in it before placing it in your aquarium.

is getting an undamaged specimen that is already attached to a rock and has no dead spots. The fan shape of this species, providing the largest surface area toward the current, has evolved to more efficiently filter the water. The polyps are normally open at night, so feeding is best done at that time. This is a Caribbean

the motion that helped give it its popular name.

Sea Whip (*Muricea muricata*)

Although this is a Caribbean species, sea whips are found throughout the tropics, usually in areas of strong water movement, and they sport all the colors of the rainbow. This is a fairly easy species to maintain. A general

small rock or coral, as this assures that its base is not damaged. The specimen should be placed in an area in the tank in which it receives plenty of current but in a spot in which the branches do not rub against a rock or piece of coral. With regular feedings of fine liquid food, specimens will often show spectacular growth.

ANEMONES: SEVERAL ORDERS

Tube Anemone (*Pachycerianthus mana*)

This member of the order Ceriantharia is an interesting animal that lives within a tube formed of mucus and detritus gained from the soft substrates to which it is adapted. It has

Another reason is that the anemone contracts into its tube quite suddenly, and thus makes itself an unsuitable host for the clownfishes. Because of this and the fact that the long stinging tentacles can be a threat to other invertebrates, the species is kept only by those

Clownfish Anemone (*Heteractis malu*)

Actually, this is only one of many anemones that clownfishes inhabit, but it is one of the most popular ones, both with the clownfishes and hobbyists. The species needs intense lighting for its symbiotic zooxanthellae. If

This sea fan, possibly *Melithaea* sp. is much more open. They are found protruding from vertical substrates in nature. Photo by Dr. H. R. Axelrod.

long, thin tentacles with a powerful sting. This is an Indo-Pacific species, but clownfishes will not adopt it for two reasons. One is that they are apparently unable to adapt to the type of stinging cells utilized by this species.

with a special interest in them. In spite of the powerful sting of the tentacles, some sea hares (giant sea slugs) prey upon these animals, and that is one reason for their quick retraction into the protecting tube!

clownfishes are kept with the anemone, it will receive plenty of food, as the clownfishes should be fed newly-hatched brine shrimp, and the anemone will prosper on that, too. It should be noted that there is a progression toward bigger food with most anemone species. Whereas corals needed very tiny planktonic animals, anemones are able to take larger prey. Nevertheless, the popular notion of anemones trapping large fishes for food are erroneous. All anemones feed upon much smaller food than that, but they

Carpet Anemone (*Stoichactis gigas*)

This is another anemone that is more suited for a tank of clownfishes. The problem is that not only does this anemone have a powerful sting, it gets to be quite large. It can be very aggressive toward other anemones, and corals, too. Not the best choice for a reef tank.

Mushroom Anemone (*Zoanthus sociatus*)

Here is an example in which an anemone is confused with a coral colony. The fact is that these show many of the characteristics of corals, and the confusion is understandable. Not only that, but this is a fairly easy species to keep. All it needs is

This clownfish anemone, *Heteractis* sp. (possibly *magnifica* or *malu*), needs intense lighting because of its symbiotic zooxanthellae. Photo by U. Erich Friese.

might opportunistically take a small fish carcass that happens to fall upon them. It should be noted that this species of anemone is of concern in the reef tank, as it can move about and be a hazard to delicate corals.

But what a species! They come in a variety of colors, from beige to green, and each of them is gorgeous. Perhaps not best for a reef tank, this is a choice species for a special tank (with the same lighting as a reef tank) with just anemones and clownfishes.

good water quality and good lighting. In good condition, mature polyps often multiply by budding new tiny polyps at the base. Most species are colored in various shades of green, brown, and beige, but several bright yellow types are occasionally seen. To add to

Zoanthids, like this *Zoanthus sociatus*, can form dense mats completely covering the bottom in shallow water. Photo by P. Colin at La Parguera, Puerto Rico.

with some of the traditional animals in a reef tank and am covering the photosynthetic animals first. This particular group of animals will be the last of the photosynthetic ones.

Giant Clams (*Tridacna* species)

These bivalves include the giant clam that have so often been portrayed as trapping a diver by the foot and drowning him. The fact is that *Tridacna gigas* does get quite large, weighing over two hundred pounds, but they don't try to trap divers. Like all healthy clams, they shut quickly if touched, and that may have been the trait that gave rise to the stories (and inevitable illustrations). The fact is that all these clams are filter feeders, feeding upon

the confusion with this species, it should be mentioned that it is often called a "mushroom coral." And, truth be told, corals and anemones are quite similar in structure and in life style to us ordinary humans, even if they are placed in separate classes by the biologists who know them best.

There are a number of *Rhodactis* and *Amplexidiscus* species of anemones which are often known as mushroom corals, too. All these species have been extremely popular among reef tank hobbyists, as they are hardy, needing primarily good water quality, and they are not too demanding with regard to light quality. Part of their popularity also stems from the bizarre variety of shapes and forms in which they are found. They are a taxonomist's delight, in that they are very difficult to identify as to species.

BIVALVES: CLASS PELECYPODA

Once again, let me remind you that we are not going in phylogenetic order (the order of evolutionary development) here, as is usually the case in listing species. In the meantime, I am proceeding

This sea anemone, *Stichodactyla haddoni*, has a characteristic bright purplish pink ring around the mouth. Photo by U. Erich Friese.

plankton, and they have little interest in divers or anything else larger than a newly-hatched brine shrimp. The mantles contain symbiotic zooxanthellae that will provide the clam with sufficient nutrition, under the proper lighting

species, such as the blue clam, *Tridacna crocea*, which are usually sold at a size of about four inches and grow to about eight inches. What's more, the blue mantle makes for a very attractive addition to the tank. Although all of these clams come from the

normally collected from around the area of Singapore, and it has a marbled pattern that may not be as flashy as the mantle of the blue clam, but it has a rich and striking appeal which many hobbyists appreciate. It reaches about a foot in width.

Heteractis magnificus can be used as a home for certain anemonefishes. Be sure to find out if the particular fishes and anemone are compatible. A mismatch could end in disaster. Photo by Burkhard Kahl.

conditions, so that feedings are only supplemental. Liquid food or newly-hatched brine shrimp can be fed on a weekly basis.

Although even *Tridacna gigas* will grow slowly in a reef tank, reef hobbyists may prefer to keep smaller

South Pacific and Indian Oceans, there is a certain amount of geographical variation as to color. Some blue clams are more intensely blue than others, and some are purplish and even green in hue. *Tridacna maxima* is

Unlike many other filter feeders, the giant clams are not at all adverse to feeding in the daytime. Some hobbyists utilize a pipette or syringe to feed the clams individually in order not to disperse either liquid food or a batch of newly-hatched

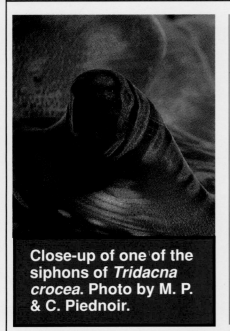

Close-up of one of the siphons of *Tridacna crocea*. Photo by M. P. & C. Piednoir.

brine shrimp all over the tank. With all the photosynthetic filter feeders we have been discussing, it is better to underfeed them than to overfeed them. So make the supplementary feedings infrequent and sparse, while keeping a good eye on your specimens. If they are looking healthy, stay open but close when touched, and are growing, they are getting ample nutrition from photosynthesis and from the supplementary feedings. For that reason, you may want to consider cutting back on the feedings slightly if your clams are all looking good. Overfeeding them won't hurt

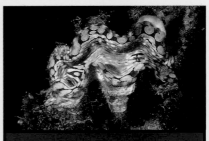

In nature *Tridacna* shells are nestled in crevices in the reef. The colorful mantle is exposed to the light. Photo by Cathy Church.

them directly, but it will compromise the quality of your water.

The mantles of *Tridacna* are all very colorful and easily spotted on the reefs. These giant clams are not dangerous to pearl divers as depicted in fictional South Sea stories. Photo by Cathy Church.

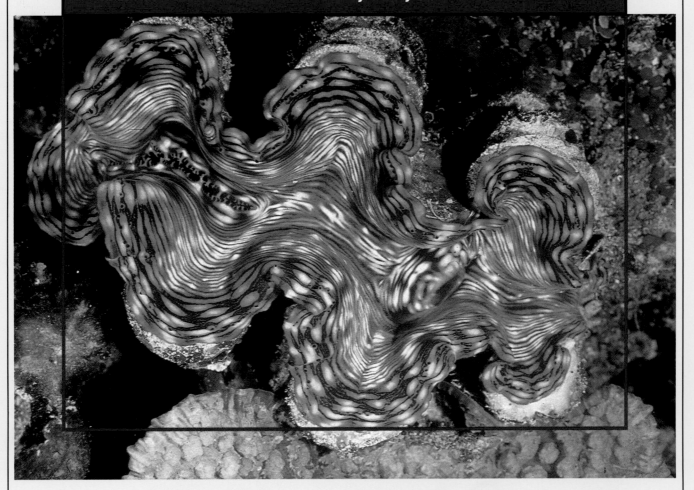

Colorful sponges are sometimes added to the reef tank but they are very chancy. Although they can literally be torn apart and survive, they can also be quite delicate in a marine aquarium. Photo by Dr. H. R. Axelrod.

NON-PHOTOSYNTHETIC ORGANISMS

The stunning new developments in lighting technology has focused the attention of the reef aquarist on maintenance of the types of organisms he was never able to keep before. Thus, attention is nearly always on corals, anemones, and other such animals that were nearly impossible to keep before because they needed nothing less than light from the sun. The ability now to supply that artificially has led to a lot of excitement about such animals, but it should be remembered that there are many other invertebrates that are also exciting to keep—and now they can be kept in a more natural habitat.

Sponges (Phylum: Porifera)

Actually, I am fudging a bit here, as many sponge species do contain species of blue-green algae that act as zooxanthellae in their "body" and that provide supplemental nutrients for them. However, the keeping of sponges is a chancy situation at present in the marine hobby. Some aquarists do very well with them; others quickly give up on them.

It is ironic that these animals are such a problem in the aquarium. They are found in oceans all over the world, including cold waters. Strictly speaking, they might be termed a colony, as the animal can be torn apart, or even run through a blender, and the cells will reconstitute themselves. There are no organs or tissues to irreparably damage. Biologists know, however, that the division between a colony and an organism is somewhat artificial. We humans have many aspects of a colony animal when viewed in a certain perspective.

In any case, even though sponges can be literally torn apart without really hurting them, they can be quite

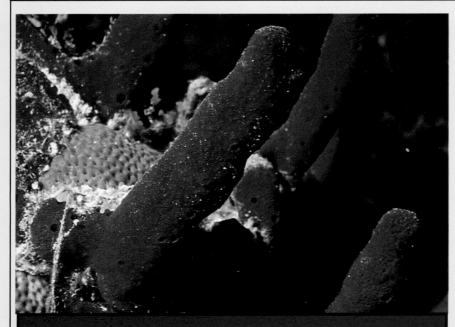

The dull red branches of this Caribbean sponge, *Haliclona rubens*, may reach 40 cm in length in their natural habitat. They arise from a basal encrusting mass. Photo by Dr. P. L. Colin, at Rio Bueno, Jamaica.

delicate in a marine situation. They need some light—at least some specimens do—for the "zooxanthellae" in their tissues; yet, if they receive too much light, they can become covered with encrusting algae which eventually kill the sponge. A few species with high levels of zooxanthellae do well in bright lighting, as they seem to have biochemical functions to prohibit algal growth.

The point is that sponges are difficult to keep, but another important fact is that aquarists who like sponges have learned to keep some of them successfully. Part of the secret is in finding exactly the correct lighting level for a given species, the correct current flow, and the proper feedings of a suitable planktonic-like food.

Sponges are without definite form, although certain species tend toward a certain shape, but it can be quite variable. Because of this fact, sponges are difficult to classify and diagnose as to species. Biologists who specialize in them usually have to examine them at the microscopic level in order to determine the species. One method of classification is through use of their spicules, the structures that support the different cells. The phylum name refers to the many pores characteristic of all sponges. Most of the nutrition of sponges is obtained by filtering water through them to a central chamber and then passing the filtered water from the sponge out though large pores called oscules. Tiny organic particles, including bacteria and elements of the plankton, are filtered and consumed. There are a few species that are found in fresh water.

This orange bread crumb sponge, *Halichondria japonica*, is being utilized as camouflage by the crab *Dromia dehaani*. Photo courtesy Takemura and Suzuki.

Red Tree Sponge (*Haliclona compressa*)

This orange to red species is very common in the Caribbean Sea, and it is one of the sponges that is most often available. The preferred specimens are six to eight inches tall, but they can grow to a much larger size. Few aquarists are going to complain about such a thing, as it means that the specimen is thriving. As with corals, it is important to get a specimen with its base attached to a piece of rock and that has not been damaged, as damaged areas can provide a breeding ground for bacteria which can eventually kill the sponge. This species needs some water flow, and it does best in somewhat dim lighting conditions. As is the case with most sponges, color and shape can be quite variable.

Blue Tubular Sponge (*Adocia* species)

Different species of this genus are regularly brought in from the Indo-Pacific region. They are popular because of the usually blue coloration and because of the fact that these are some of the more hardy sponges. If they receive subdued lighting, regular feedings of liquid invertebrate foods, and a moderate to mild current, sponges of this genus generally prosper and grow, often developing new "branches."

Flatworms (Phylum Platyhelminthes)

Most flatworms would not

Adocia carbonaria is consistently blackish in color, a character that can be helpful in its identification. This Caribbean sponge occurs in reef areas as well as turtle grass beds. Photo by Dr. P. L. Colin.

be of interest to the marine hobbyist. Some are introduced with live rock, but they don't last long without a food supply. However, there are a few large species that have an esthetic appeal and will do well in established reef tanks in which they can find microscopic material on which to dine.

Red-rimmed Flatworm (*Pseudoceros splendidus*)

The bright colors of this species are believed to serve as a warning to potential predators that they are mildly toxic to eat and, at the very best, are foul tasting. Although fishes will usually leave them alone because of their unappetizing smell and taste, some crabs will attack them on general principles, and some will even eat them. Of course, beauty is in the eye of the beholder, but many hobbyists like this species. Even so, it is rarely seen. A saving grace is that it is not nocturnal, as are so many species of flatworms, so, at

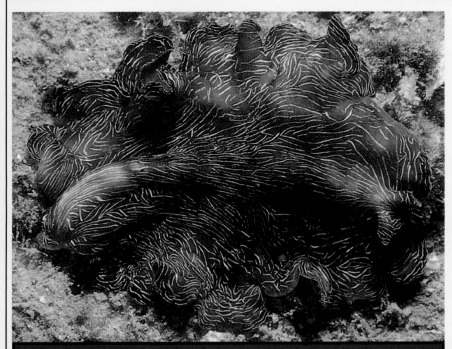

Some flatworms are very attractive and will thrive in a mini-reef situation provided it can be supplied with a sufficient amount of the proper food. This is a species of *Pseudoceros* from Oman. Photo by T. Woodward.

This is a different species of *Pseudoceros* from Hawaii. Flatworms sometimes enter a hobbyist's tank on the living rock, but they may also be purchased from your dealer. Photo by Stan Jazwinski.

least it will be out in the light displaying its rich coloration. Individuals of this species are believed to scavenge off microscopic animals found in tiny bits of detritus. It reaches a length of about two inches.

Yellow-spotted Flatworm (*Thysanozoon flavomaculatum*)

This species hails from the Red Sea, and its attractive coloration makes it a welcome bonus that occasionally comes in with live rock imported from that area. The Red Sea is a special place with special animals unique to that area. This may be one of the rarest animals to be seen in tanks in this country, but its very uniqueness adds to its appeal. If not subjected to predation, it normally thrives in a reef tank and reaches a length of about two inches.

Segmented Worms (Phylum Annelida)

The familiar earthworms belong to this phylum. However, the phylum would not be recognizable to other than biologists in the forms it takes in the ocean. The sea cousins to the lowly earthworm have made some remarkable adaptations and are often creatures of exquisite beauty. Unfortunately, some of these beautiful (appreciation of their beauty may be an acquired taste!) creatures may only be seen when they emerge from some secret hiding place and spew eggs through the water (much to the delight of the filter feeders!).

The best Christmas tree worms seem to come in with *Porites* coral. This is *Spirobranchus gigantea* from the Caribbean. Photo by M. P. & C. Piednoir.

aforementioned one. Like it, it hails from the Indian Ocean, and it has all the virtues of the other species. The only possible dilemma caused by these species is that of providing a substrate for them. Most reef tank keepers don't maintain a substrate. That is the simple approach. No one knows the difference, because all the live rock and corals cover up the bottom area anyway, and the aquarist doesn't have to worry about the build-up of anaerobic bacteria in the gravel. A possible solution is to provide a natural looking container with a bit

A gorgeous flatworm, *Pseudoceros sp.* Many types of large flatworms live on and near the reef. Photo by R. Steene.

Fanworm (*Sebellastarte magnifica*)

Here is a creature with all the requirements for popularity among the reef tank hobbyists. It is so bizarre as to resemble a creature from another planet, and yet it has an eerie beauty. The body of the worm is encased in a parchment tube buried in the substrate, with the feathery head extended for feeding. At the approach of danger, the feathery tentacles are very rapidly withdrawn into the tube. They are not fussy about their lighting requirements, they can even cope with sub-par water conditions (but should not have to do so!), and they are easily satisfied with a simple filter-feeder food mix.

Featherduster Worm (*Sebellastarte sanctijosephi*)

This species is quite similar to the

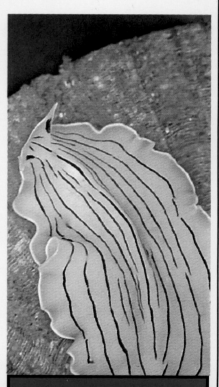

The lined flatworm, *Prostheceraeus vittatus* of the North Atlantic can be adapted to cooler aquatia. Photo by Dr. T. E. Thompson.

of sand for the featherduster worm. Some hobbyists will have circumvented the problem by maintaining gravel in the tank, along with reverse flow filtration. This make things a little more complicated, but it is a system that generally works out well.

These species not infrequently spawn in the home aquarium. When this is about to happen, the first signs are usually evident early in the morning, when the animals emit smoky plumes of either eggs or sperm. The adult worms normally shed their feathery head appendages. This is believed to be an adaptation that keeps the parents from eating their own larvae, but it may just be a part of the process of "clearing the decks for action," as the worms also shed the feathers if attacked by predators. If left alone, after two or three weeks a new feathery head will reappear and eventually grow back to its full size.

Christmas Tree Worm (*Spirobranchus giganteus*)
This is a spectacular species if you are lucky

Featherduster worms, like this *Sabellastarte sanctijosephi*, attract a lot of attention. But do not make a sudden move or they will disappear into their tubes lightning fast. Photo by W. Deas.

enough to get some of them. The best specimens come in with *Porites* coral, as the animals imbed their tubes in the coral (and that saves us the problem of worrying about a substrate!). The species is aptly named, as the "feathers" which protrude to extract plankton are in spirals of decreasing size, giving a decided Christmas tree appearance. This species hails from the Caribbean, and it should be placed in a position of lower lighting so that it is not encrusted by algae.

Bristleworms (*Hermodice carunculata*)

Although this species has a certain beauty, it is the bane of the reef tank hobbyists. Actually, there are several species of bristleworms. There are two major problems with them. They are painful to handle with bare hands, as the fluffy-looking tufts along the sides are, in fact, extremely painful needle-sharp calcium spicules. Also, they are disgustingly fecund, and they can easily reproduce in the reef tank. Most hobbyists remove them whenever they see them, using either gloved hands or tongs for handling them. Although hated by most reef tankers, the many species of bristleworms are very interesting, and some hobbyists actually keep them on purpose! However, they give them a tank of their own. They feed on detritus, so their numbers should stay small in a properly cared for reef

Viewed from the side, it is no wonder that these animals are called Christmas tree worms. This is *Spirobranchus* sp. (possibly *grandis*). Photo by Cathy Church.

The calcareous tube of this serpulid worm can be seen through the feathery head appendages. Photo by Courtney Platt.

A cluster of the serpulid worm *Spirobranchus giganteus* growing on a sponge, probably *Neofibularia nolitangere*. There is also a brittle star in their midst. Photo by P. Colin.

The fire worm, *Hermodice carunculata*, is well named. The fluffy-looking tufts along the sides are extremely sharp calcium spicules able to cause a great deal of pain to a person who unknowingly picks up the worm. Photo by P. Colin.

tank. But hobbyists still remove them whenever they spot them. In this era of especially cultivated live rock, the problem of bristleworms should eventually become an historical one.

CRABS, LOBSTERS, AND BARNACLES (PHYLUM CRUSTACEA)

This group consists of some of the most charming and beguiling of reef inhabitants. It also includes animals, such as the mantis shrimp, which have no place in the living reef tank, but somehow often end up there—much to the exasperation of the hobbyist! Often, though, the charm and beauty of a reef tank is topped off by a display of how a favorite crab will take food from its keeper's fingers.

Arrow Crab (*Stenorhynchus seticornis*)

The arrow crab is not being listed first under crustaceans simply because of alphabetical order. It has much to recommend it, not the least of which is the fact that it will eat bristleworms! It gets its common name from the distinctly triangular, arrowhead-shaped body. This feature, together with its very long thin legs, gives an impression of a giant spider. It gets to be about six inches, counting the long legs, but it is not considered a threat to corals, as its specialty is eating burrowing worms. Those reef tankers keeping featherduster worms in their tank may want to exclude this species, as it will go after them, too. All in all, this is a desirable species in that it is easy to maintain and has a pleasing "personality." One of the few drawbacks to the arrow crab is that it is a little large for some tanks. The species is quite

Anemone Crab (*Neopetrolisthes ohshimai*)

This Indo-Pacific crab is one of a small group of porcelain crabs that have evolved an immunity to anemone stings and, like clownfishes, can live among the tentacles of various large anemones and thus

The crabs live in the same types of anemones as clownfishes and will use their well-developed claws on any clownfish that tries to evict them; however, the clownfishes are not as aggressive toward them as they are toward species that tend to feed upon the

The arrow crab, *Stenorhynchus seticornis*, has much to recommend it. Not only is it distinctly shaped, but it will eat bristle worms as well! Photo by Mike Mesgleski.

territorial in regard to others of its species, so only one should be kept to a tank, unless the tank is very large or there are natural dividers isolating each arrow crab.

receive protection from predators. They measure barely an inch across the carapace, and they are surely among the best of the crabs as potential reef candidates.

anemone. The anemone crab feeds upon small particulate matter, including plankton, and it may help keep the anemone clean by scavenging debris from among the tentacles.

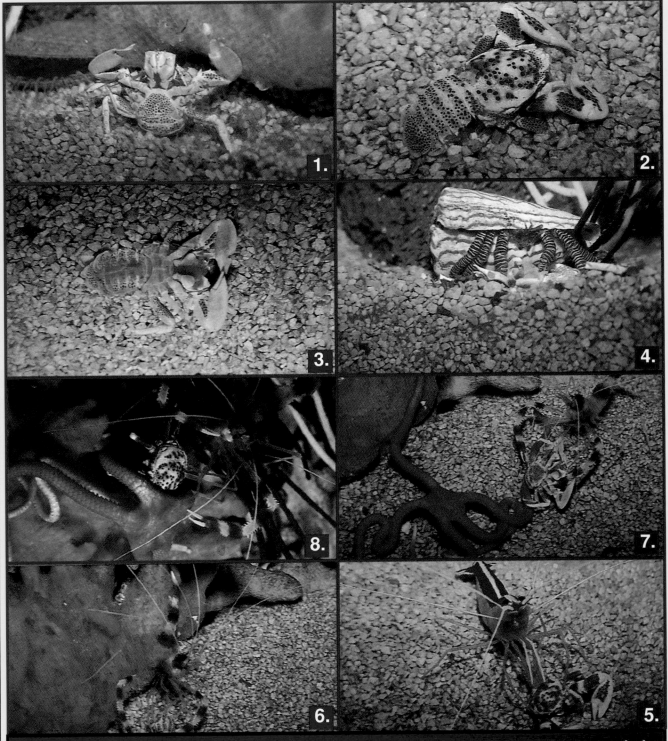

1-3. Different views of the porcelain crab, *Neopetrolisthes ohshimai* (abdomen curled under, abdomen stretched out, and ventral view). 4. This hermit crab, *Aniculus strigatus*, has found a cone shell to serve as its home until such time as he outgrows it. 5. Interaction between the porcelain crab, *Neopetrolisthes ohshimai*, and a cleaning shrimp, *Lysmata amboinensis*. 6-8. Apparent attack on the porcelain crab by another cleaning shrimp, *Stenopus hispidus*. The brittle-star may just be a curious bystander. Photos by J. Kelly Giwojna.

The crab has small feathery projections on its jaw processes to process particulate matter. As is the case with most crustaceans, the anemone crab is particularly vulnerable to predation right after it has molted, that is, shed its carapace; hence, hiding places are needed if you aren't keeping it with a suitable anemone.

There are several other species of this genus and family that are also suitable for the reef aquarium.

Boxing Crab (*Lybia tessellata*)

This little crab has to be in the running for the most charming—and most bizarre—of all animals. This crab barely reaches an inch in length. Still, it is not a fellow to be trifled with. These small crabs collect a tiny anemone in each claw and actively wave them at encroaching predators as a warning (the boxing effect). So we see that not only is the boxing crab a tool using animal, but it utilizes a most unusual tool: living anemones. When the crab sheds its exoskeleton, it carefully puts the anemones down, setting them aside until the new shell hardens. Then the anemones are picked up once again and pressed into service.

The boxing crab is not fussy as to food and is one of the species that will take food from the fingers of its keeper. There are many suitable species of boxing crabs that make good reef residents, and nearly all of

This Fijian boxing crab, *Lybia edmondsoni*, is hanging on tightly to its anemones (*Triactis producta*), ready to ward off any potential enemies. Photo by Bruce Carlson.

Lybia tessellata in its natural habitat. This one comes from the Hawaiian Islands and is barely an inch long. Photo by Scott Johnson.

Porcelain crabs, like this *Neopetrolisthes ohshimai*, have developed an immunity to anemone stings and can live in the protection of their tentacles. Photo by Aaron Norman.

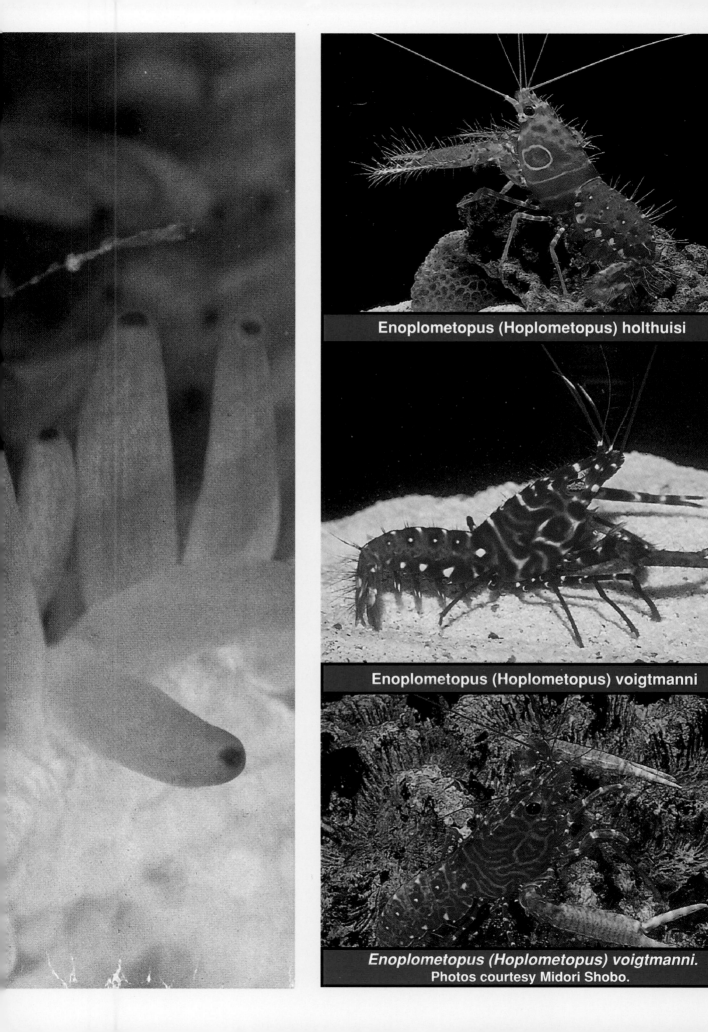

Enoplometopus (Hoplometopus) holthuisi

Enoplometopus (Hoplometopus) voigtmanni

Enoplometopus (Hoplometopus) voigtmanni.
Photos courtesy Midori Shobo.

The red dwarf lobster, *Enoplometopus (Hoplometopus) occidentalis*, is a good scavenger but is also predatory on crabs and may even grab fishes at night while they are sleeping. Photo by Burkhard Kahl.

them are in the genus *Lybia*. All of them are not only comical, but they are quite interesting to observe and have a fascinating life history.

Red Dwarf Lobster (*Enoplometopus occidentalis*)

Most of us are primarily familiar with the lobster species that we use for food, and, of course, those are much to big for a reef aquarium. This species only reaches a size of about four inches, but it is still a questionable candidate for the reef tank. It is a good scavenger, but it is also predatory on crabs and may seize fishes at night when they are sleeping. It will defend its territory from other species of lobster, so this truly is a questionable species in spite of its charm. Nevertheless, there are situations in which it could be a suitable reef inhabitant. For example, a hobbyist who was keeping a tank of large anemones, clownfishes, and some of the anemone crabs would not have to worry about a specimen of this species harming any of those animals.

Another lobster species that is a possible candidate is the purple spiny lobster, *Panulirus versicolor*, which has spines or antennae in place of the large claws. It reaches a size of about eight inches and is not as predatory as the red dwarf lobster, but it can do accidental damage, just because of its size. All lobsters seem to be easily startled, and, when they are, they shoot backwards with a quick flip of the tail and other appendages. Just a maneuver such as that could cause damage to some of the more delicate corals.

The hobbyist who wants to keep any of the lobster species must take into account that most of them are going to hide during the day anyway since they are nocturnal (although, to be honest, most can be coaxed out with food). And once you put a specimen in and it creates any sort of problem, you are going to have a devil of a time getting it out. Plan on a general dismantling of the tank in order to remove a specimen.

Coral-banded Shrimp (*Stenopus hispidus*)

Here is a species that has all the advantages of a lobster and a very similar appearance, but it doesn't have any of the drawbacks. First of all, it only attains a size of about two inches. It stays out in the open in the daytime (once it has become accustomed to the tank), and it is compatible with other species of shrimp. (However, it may fight with other members of its own species, although it is possible to get a compatible pair.) It has personality and will gesticulate and wave for attention with its claws. It is a hardy eater and a good scavenger. As is the case with most crustaceans, it is quite vulnerable after it has shed its exoskeleton and,

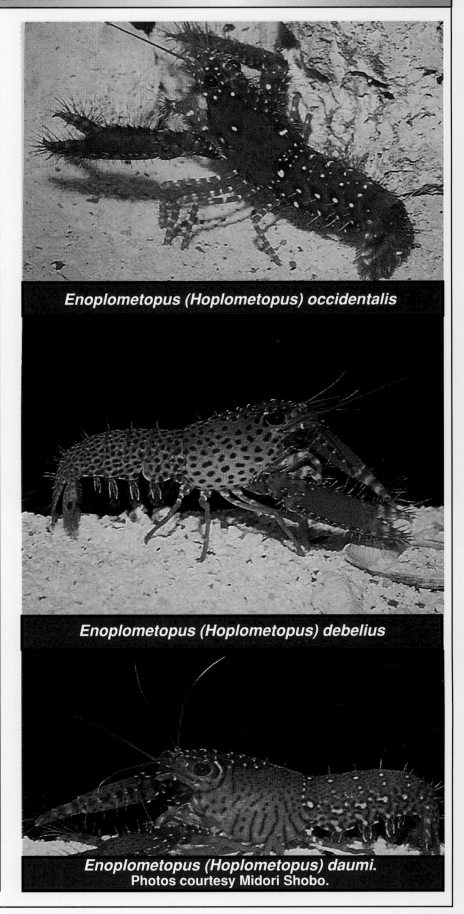

Enoplometopus (Hoplometopus) occidentalis

Enoplometopus (Hoplometopus) debelius

Enoplometopus (Hoplometopus) daumi.
Photos courtesy Midori Shobo.

These are fresh or brackish water crabs of the genus *Paratelphusa* and cannot be added to a reef tank. The male is the smaller, dark colored animal. Photo by Rodney Jonklaas.

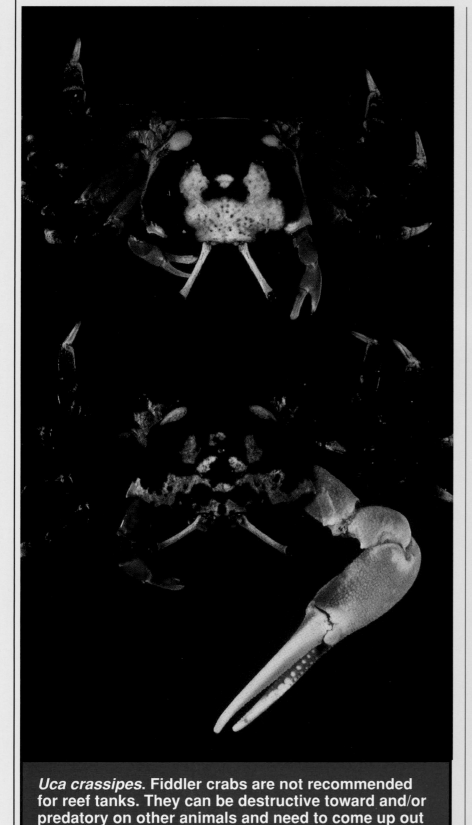

Uca crassipes. Fiddler crabs are not recommended for reef tanks. They can be destructive toward and/or predatory on other animals and need to come up out of the water. Kept separately and provided with a sandy "beach" they make interesting pets.

The coral-banded shrimp or candy cane shrimp (*Stenopus hispidus*) is a cleaner shrimp and will remove parasites and dead flesh from fishes that present themselves for cleaning. The long white antennae are said to advertise their "services." Photo by Courtney Platt.

Stenopus hispidus gets along well with most other shrimp but tends to squabble with its own species, possibly leading to the demise of one of the two. Photo by Dr. Herbert R. Axelrod.

Lysmata amboinensis is also a cleaning shrimp. It will actually try to groom the aquarist's finger if placed in the tank.

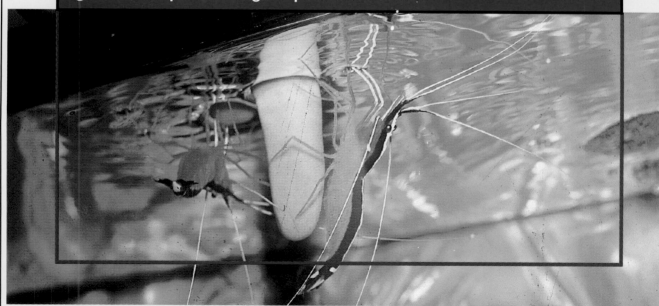

thus, should have plenty of hiding places into which it can retreat while its new carapace hardens.

Cleaner Shrimp (*Lysmata amboinensis*)

Not only is this a good-looking species, but it is particularly interesting because it is involved with cleaning symbiosis, almost a trademark of the ocean. The common name for these very attractive and sociable shrimps comes from their natural cleaning behavior. In the wild, on Indo-Pacific reefs, they will pick parasites from many species of fishes, including large groupers and moray eels.

This species is long lived in the aquarium and a group of five or so can be kept amicably together; they will even spawn in the reef aquarium. The females develop large quantities of green eggs under their abdomen. Raising the pelagic young is another matter. It could probably be done in a tank kept just for that purpose, but, in the reef tank, the tiny pelagic young are simply

part of the menu of filter feeders.

Candy Shrimp (*Rhynchocinetes uritai*)

Here is another attractive shrimp that is best kept in a group of about five or so. Single specimens tend to hide most of the time. This shrimp only reaches a length of about an inch and is quite defenseless against other

Lysmata amboinensis is long lived in the aquarium and a group of four or five can be kept amicably in an aquarium. They may even spawn! Photo by C. W. Emmens.

aggressive crustaceans. This species is quite hardy, easy to keep, and can generally be trusted with the corals and other reef animals. These traits, combined with their impressive appearance makes them excellent candidates for the reef tank.

Harlequin Shrimp (*Hymenocera picta*)

This species is often offered for sale and is nearly

irresistible, as it is quite gorgeous. In fact, they are sometimes sold as pairs by dealers. As such, they certainly make a nice display. Unfortunately, they are very specialized feeders, dining solely on starfish. Hence, unless you have a supply of these animals for feeding purposes, your harlequins will simply starve to death.

In view of the fact that we have occasional plagues of crown-of-thorns starfish that decimate coral areas, it would seem that these animals could be collected and frozen for use as food. While we are not in favor of decimating any species, surely over-populated species that are doing harm could be used as food. (Of course, I am well aware that the same argument could be made in regard to *Homo sapiens*!)

Anemone Shrimp (*Periclimenes imperator*)

There are several species of anemone shrimp, but most of them are transparent or sport colors that make them difficult to spot. They live among the protective corals of anemones, much like clownfishes and anemone crabs. This species hails from the Red Sea and Indian Ocean, and it is most often crimson with a white pattern over the top, although coloration does vary even in the species. It reaches a length of only an inch and should not be kept in the same anemone with other crustaceans, such as the anemone crab.

Mantis Shrimp (*Odontodactylus* species)

Many of these species are quite colorful, and they certainly do have personality. However...they are listed here more as a warning than anything else. They are a reef keeper's worst nightmare. They are fierce predators, taking fishes, corals, and just about anything else you have in your tank. To top it off, they are known unaffectionately as "thumbsplitters" by fishermen. That nickname tells you that they can even do damage to the hobbyist. And just when you think things couldn't be worse, they are! If you try to catch a specimen that has once gotten into your tank, you will find yourself chasing a veritable will-o'-the-wisp, as these things can seemingly tunnel right through solid rock. (Actually, that is an exaggeration, but they can certainly tunnel through coral.)

Although these specimens have no place in a reef tank, they are of sufficient interest that they

The anemone shrimp or emperor shrimp, *Periclimenes imperor*, feeds on its host's mucus and anything edible it can reach from it. The host is the *nudibranch Ceratosoma cornigerum*. Photo by Dr. Leon P. Zann.

This emperor shrimp is well camouflaged on its host, the Spanish dancer *Hexabranchus sanguineus*. Photo by Aaron Norman.

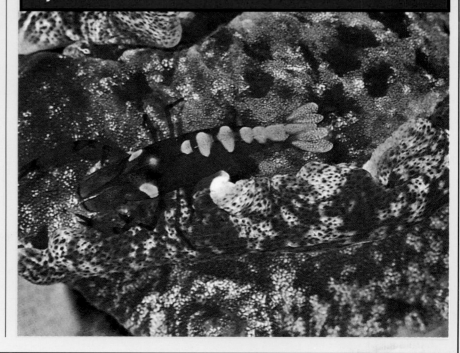

One of the prettiest shrimp is the harlequin shrimp, *Hymenocera picta*. This specimen apparently came off second best in a fight and has lost its claws! Photo by Aaron Norman.

would make a not uninteresting display in a tank of their own.

SEA SNAILS, SEA SLUGS, AND CEPHALOPODS (PHYLUM MOLLUSCA)

Tiger Cowry (*Cypraea tigris*)

This is a species whose shell is well known to shell collectors. Unfortunately, the demand for the shells of these animals have put intensive pressure upon their populations in Singapore and the Philippines, where desperately poor and overpopulated humans are

Mantis shrimp are not recommended for the reef tank. They are fierce predators that can even do damage to the hobbyist. This "thumbsplitter" is *Hemisquilla ensigera*. (The fish is a young garibaldi, *Hypsypops rubicunda*). Photo by G. Wolfsheimer.

A close-up of the head end of a mantis shrimp, in this case *Odontodactylus scyllarus*. Although these animals have no place in the reef tank, they are often kept in a tank of their own by interested aquarists. Photo by Burkhard Kahl.

The tiger cowry, *Cypraea tigris*, is well known to shell collectors but only seldom is seen for sale alive. It is easy to keep, but has quite an appetite — that may extend to your corals! Photos by Alan Power.

perfectly willing to go out and collect the animals for their shells. This means that the species may not always be available to marine hobbyists. This species is usually about three inches long, and it is easy to keep, but it is a questionable inhabitant for the reef tank, as one of the reasons for its hardiness is its appetite. And that may extend to corals!

Queen Conch (*Strombus gigas*)

The only drawback to this species is that it will attain a large size, easily surpassing a foot in length. Fortunately, it takes quite a while for it to reach such a size. In the meantime, it will help keep your tank clean of algae and will further serve as a scavenger. Since this animal is popular in the Caribbean as a food item, there are regulations about harvesting small ones, so it is not easy to obtain wild-caught ones for the aquarium. However, they are one of the marine animals that is farmed, so small farmed specimens are

The queen conch (*Strombus gigas*) will keep your tank clean of algae and serve as a scavenger as well. But it does attain a large size. Photo by Courtney Platt.

readily available. If they aren't on display, just ask your dealer to order it for you. As one who kept this species thirty years ago, I can attest to its hardiness. My specimen was about an inch long and had grown to about two inches in a year's time. After five years, it was about six inches long, so you can gauge how long you can keep your specimen by figuring about an inch a year in growth.

Sea Cones (*Conus* species)

These species are listed as a cautionary measure: to let you know what you are in for if you get one of these animals. First of all, they are efficient fish predators, harpooning them with a deadly dart. In some

species this same "dart" (which is a specially adapted radular tooth contained in the cone's proboscis) that immobilizes the fish can easily kill a person. The poison is a nerve toxin similar to that secreted by many cobras.

Now, there are people who keep sea cones (but there are people who keep cobras, too!), but they are only interesting as a display in the act of predation. The rest of the time is spent underneath the gravel in the tank. Obviously, this is not a species for the reef tank. (If one gets in your reef tank,

send a mantis shrimp in to get it! But them you have to get the mantis shrimp out again!)

Sea Hare (*Aplysia datylomela*)

Although there are several species of sea hare and many of them are of colorful hues, they are similar in that they primarily eat vegetable matter. For that reason, they are the only nudibranch that is suitable for the reef aquarium. Other species have extremely specialized diets, often feeding upon coral

Certain cone shells can be dangerous not only to the animals in a tank but to the aquarist as well. *Conus bartschi* from the west coast of Mexico is a worm eater and not among those that are deadly to larger animals. Photo by Alex Kerstitch.

Species of *Acropora* produce a lot of mucus and are not easy to raise. Photo by M.P. & C. Piednoir.

The sea hares, like this *Aplysia californica*, will happily take care of all of your algal problems — including hair algae. Photo by Mark Smith.

Sea hares not only glide over the substrate, they can "flap their wings and fly." Although this means of transportation is somewhat awkward, it gets them where they want to go. Photo of *Aplysia californica* by Aaron Norman.

polyps. I have kept many species of sea slugs and nudibranchs, hoping to be able to substitute something for their natural prey which they would eat. But they simply followed their instincts, combing the tank for the only food that they recognized as such. The sea hare gets its common name from their ear-like projections, resembling superficially a rabbit's ear. Eventually, most species of sea hare will get too large for reef tanks. In the meantime, they will happily take care of all your algae problems, including growths of hair algae.

Octopus (*Octopus cyaneus*)

This is a species of octopus which is one of the most common of the tropical species. It stays relatively small, with a maximum arm span of about 12 inches; however, no octopus is a truly good candidate for the reef tank. That is, they are not good candidates if you are going to keep crustaceans and fishes in your reef tank. They are a great temptation, however, as they are one of the emblems of the sea, and they are one of the most intelligent of the invertebrates. Ethologists (animal behavior researchers) can't resist them, and they have discovered that species of octopus can actually learn from watching each other. Octopuses prey upon crustaceans and will opportunistically take fishes. (Some fishes prey

No octopus is a truly good candidate for a reef tank, but they are hard to resist. *Octopus cyaneus* is a common tropical species that stays relatively small. Remember, octopuses eat crustaceans. Photo by Michio Goto, Marine Life Documents.

upon octopuses, such as the moray eel, but you wouldn't keep any of them in a reef tank.)

Octopuses will take a variety of foods, including bits of clam. Gravid females will actually lay eggs in the tank in the darkest cave they can find and will tend them, keeping them clean and oxygenated by blowing water over them with their siphon tube. Unfortunately, the female dies soon after the young hatch, but the young can be raised with diligence on the part of the hobbyist.

Even without crustaceans or fishes in the tank, octopuses are of questionable character for the marine tank. If they are frightened, they may jet through the tank, using the siphon tube for propulsion, and smash into the soft corals and injure them in that way. Also, if frightened, they may give out a squirt of ink. This does not function as a smoke screen as so many people think. When the octopus jets away from a predator, it evacuates a blob of ink as a false target to confuse and distract its nemesis. Unfortunately, such a blast of ink can be lethal to corals. Obviously, an important point is not to have the octopus become frightened. The fact is that,

Octopus vulgarus **is the common octopus from the Caribbean. Like other octopuses, they are very intelligent, quickly learning how to escape your tank. Photo by Burkhard Kahl.**

fierce predators and need super-quality water, with lots of oxygenation.

PHYLUM ECHINODERMATA

Crinoids, Starfish, Sea Urchins, and Sea Cucumbers

The echinoderms are characterized by radial symmetry and a tough outer skin; in fact, echinoderm means spiny skin. It is of interest that we and all the other vertebrates are included with echinoderms in the superphylum Deuterostomia. All the animals in the superphylum are similar in that they have a dorsal nerve structure and the muscles are partially

once settled down, the animals become quite tame and will even take food from their keeper's fingers. In fact, they become so tame they will practically crawl up into your lap! Still, the dangers to a reef tank should be kept in mind. It may be that you will want to have a separate tank for an octopus. They like the same high quality water as is needed in a reef tank, but prefer dark hiding places to well lit areas.

Incidentally, the plural of octopus is not "octopi." The name comes from Greek, not from Latin.

Other cephalopods, such as the cuttlefish (*Sepia plangon*), are extremely interesting occupants for a tank, but they are not really for the reef tank either, as they are also

Some octopuses are quite pretty. This *Octopus ornatus* from Hawaii is nicely patterned with white spots. Photo by Scott Johnson.

actuated by creatine phosphate. Not every scientist agrees with this grouping, but it is interesting to ponder that we are a little more closely related to these animals than any other invertebrate!

Red Crinoid (*Himerometra robustipinna*)

Crinoids are sometimes called feather starfish. However, they are able to move around much faster than starfishes, and they are a spectacular and alien-looking animal. They are nocturnal in their natural habitat, finding little crevasses in the coral to hide out in the daytime, but emerge at night to extend their feathery arms to entrap plankton and other tiny particulate organic matter. In the reef tank, they fit in perfectly, as they will feed on the same diet as most corals and at the same time, too. Not having photosynthetic zooxanthellae, they need more frequent feedings than corals, anemones, or clams. A pipette or syringe can be used to direct food just at them, as they should be fed at least three times a week. It will be found that some of the shrimp will hide in the crinoid, much like they would in an anemone. This won't hurt the crinoid, and it is quite common in nature. However, many crabs and some fishes will do harm to a crinoid by picking at it. Arms that break off are regenerated as long as the species is prospering in the tank.

Beautiful and fascinating in a reef tank, the red crinoid does have the disadvantages of being nocturnal and delicate in the sense that it is easy to damage. Still, suitable tank mates will solve the latter problem, and a few daytime feedings will help bring the crinoid out at that time, thus allowing visitors to view its splendor.

The red crinoid, *Himerometra robustipinna*, is beautiful and fascinating, but it is nocturnal and easy to damage. Choosing suitable tank mates and coaxing it out during the daytime will help avoid these drawbacks. Photo by Dr. G. R. Allen.

Crinoids are much more mobile than most other echinoderms and can wander about the tank. But they like to sit on top of a coral head at night and wave their arms searching for planktonic tidbits. Photo of *Himerometra* sp. by Dr. Herbert R. Axelrod.

Ophiomastix mixta **is one of the few venomous brittlestars known. The large spines on the arms carry the poison. Photo by Takemura and Susuki.**

A commensal brittlestar, Ophiothrix (Acanthophiothrix) sp., living in a Dendronephthya host. Photo by Dr. Leon P. Zann.

Brittle Starfish (*Ophiomastix venosa*)

Although the brittle starfish doesn't match our idea of what a starfish "should" look like, it has more personality than most of the others because of the fact that it moves around more rapidly and quickly comes out of hiding when food is placed in the tank. They are of particular value in the reef tank because they are scavengers, and they will help keep debris cleaned out of the many crevices that are invariably found in such a tank.

There are many species of brittle starfish. This one comes from the Caribbean, and it is frequently found in association with sea urchins, utilizing the protection of the spines. As might be supposed, the popular name comes from the propensity of such species to easily drop an arm if "trapped." Such arms normally regenerate; however, such "trauma" should be avoided, as too many incidents would most definitely take a toll on the animal.

Blue Starfish (*Linckia laevigata*)

What is more suggestive of the sea than a starfish? Many people have never seen one alive, but everyone has seen the dried-out bodies of various species that are sold around the world. It speaks highly of the success of all of the various species that the sea has not been completely denuded of them, as almost every child has been given one of these

The blue starfish, *Linckia laevigata*, has been used as a dried decoration in many marine motifs. But it can also be a colorful living addition to a reef tank. It feeds well and will even scavenge. Photo courtesy C. L. I.

at least once, and they are a staple of all shell collections—even though they aren't a shell. I well remember, many decades ago, a fellow wading out into the ocean at low tide and coming back with over twenty starfish stacked like pancakes. He would unload them in a basket and return for more. That was before any sort of era of conservation had begun, but I remember feeling somewhat resentful of the waste of all those animals just to decorate that guy's yard. (In retrospect, though, he was probably selling them dried once they had cured.) Although

there are still plenty of starfishes in the ocean, it is not possible to collect them in the manner that was just mentioned.

This species is undoubtedly one of the most dramatically colored of all the invertebrates, and the blue coloration makes a nice contrast in the reef tank to offset the many reds. To add to its desirability, this species is often available and it is easy to keep. It feeds well and will scavenge, but many hobbyists simply place a bit of clam under the animal to speed up the process. This species won't sprint from one end of the

tank to the other to get food as a brittle star will! The species hails from the Indo-Pacific, as so many of the desirable species do, and it primarily scavenges in its natural habitat. So not only will the species earn its keep by displaying in the daytime, it will help keep the tank picked up, too!

Red Starfish (*Fromia elegans*)

This bright red species will help set off the blue starfish in coloration, and it has the added advantage that it is also readily available and reaches only a small maximum size,

Protoreaster nodosus is fairly common in the shallow waters of the Indian Ocean. Photo by K. Knaack.

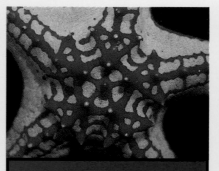

Close-up of disc of *Protoreaster nodosus* showing the intricate pattern. Photo by K. Knaack.

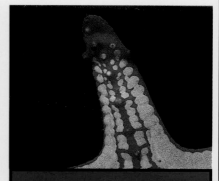

Close-up of tip of arm of *Protoreaster nodosus*. Photo by K. Knaack.

usually maturing at about three inches across. Juveniles have black tips to the arms, but these disappear with maturation. The red starfish is not a threat to corals or other sessile invertebrates. It

will happily dine upon bits of shrimp and shellfish. It should be kept in mind that all small starfishes are endangered by predatory crabs or even large predatory starfishes.

Yellow Starfish (*Fromia monilis*)

If you want to keep starfishes, you might as well have variety in coloration! This species varies from yellow to orange

Three different color patterns of *Pateria miniata*. Aquarists will commonly seek out color variations of the same species. They make good conversation pieces. Photo by Dr. Herbert R. Axelrod.

This red *Linckia columbiae* comes from the tropical Pacific Ocean. Its bright red color makes a nice contrast to the blue starfish. Photo by A. Mancini.

look the specimen over for parasites. (Most knowledgeable and reputable dealers are going to do that anyway.) Starfishes like good water quality, although some species tolerate sub-par water better than others. The species mentioned are hardy but do require good water quality.

Common Sea Urchin (*Echinometra mathaei*)

Actually, this particular species is only common in dealer's tanks. That is, it is not really the most common sea urchin species, but it is abundant in the Indo-Pacific area and frequently collected. It is a

and usually have shades of each. It is very similar in habits and diet to the prior-mentioned species. It is hardy and an excellent resident for the reef tank. It might be worthwhile at this point to mention that

***Tamaria megaloplax* has lost some of its arms but is in the process of regenerating them. Some species may reproduce asexually by deliberately breaking off their arms. Photo by Dr. Herbert R. Axelrod.**

The red starfish, *Fromia elegans*, usually matures at only about 3 inches across. Photo by Alan Power.

one of the great secrets to success with starfishes is to obtain good specimens to begin with. Healthy specimens are eager eaters and have a good tone. Limp bodies are not a good sign. Also, have the dealer

good candidate for the reef tank, as it only reaches a diameter of about four inches. Also, the spines are more short and blunt than many species, but the hobbyist must still be cautious when handling

This species of *Goniaster* is not brightly colored but is still very attractively patterned. Photo by Dr. Herbert R. Axelrod.

A species of *Protoreaster*. Photo by Dr. Herbert R. Axelrod.

A species of *Culcita* from Mombassa. Photo by Dr. Herbert R. Axelrod.

Fromia monilis with a contrasty pattern. Photo by Dr. Herbert R. Axelrod.

Fromia monilis with more subdued colors. Photo by Dr. Herbert R. Axelrod.

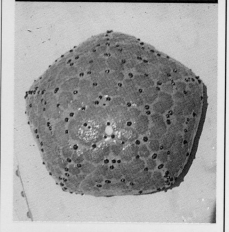

A species of *Asterias* from New Jersey, top view. Photo by Dr. Herbert R. Axelrod.

The New Jersey *Asterias* as seen from the bottom. Photo by Dr. Herbert R. Axelrod.

The Mombassa *Culcita* viewed from the bottom. Photo by Dr. Herbert R. Axelrod.

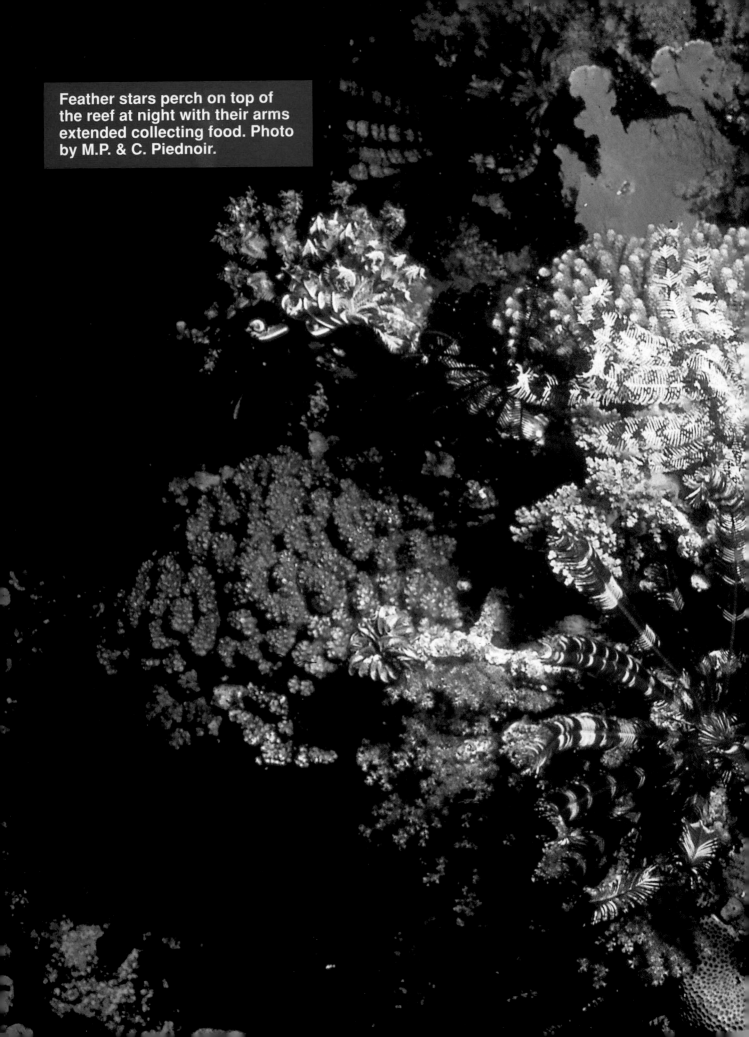

Feather stars perch on top of the reef at night with their arms extended collecting food. Photo by M.P. & C. Piednoir.

The common sea urchin, *Echinometra mathaei*, is a good candidate for the reef tank, reaching a diameter of only four inches and the spines are short and blunt. Photo by Alan Power.

them. One of the problems with sea urchins is that they tend to hide out during the day, usually in the darkest cave available. Still, they are so unusual, and they are of sufficient interest biologically, that they are worth keeping. When they are out, you can be sure that visitors will ask about them. Fortunately, several different specimens can be kept, either of the same species or of varying species, and at least one is going to be on view at any particular time.

Club Urchin (*Hetercentrotus mammillatus*)

Named club urchin because of the blunt short spines, this is one of the more unusual looking sea urchins, so naturally it is highly prized. Like most sea urchins, it feeds on algae, and its diet can be supplemented with bits of lettuce. The Ancient Egyptians used the spines of this species to write on slate, as they did the job nearly as well as chalk.

Long-spined Sea Urchin (*Diadema savignyi*)

This is the species that might more properly be called common. They seem to be of the type that is most often seen at night in the oceans all over the world. Naturally, this is a tropical species, as a temperate species would not do well in a tropical reef tank. The spines of this species are particularly painful, and scuba divers frequently hack up specimens they find, partly to attract fishes, but also in revenge for the times they may have been "spined" by such specimens in the past.

This species is recommended for the reef tank with a cautionary note. The very long spines could conceivably do damage to corals and anemones. I have never known this to happen, but I have heard of one of these guys taking a tumble during a night foray and

Heterocentrotus mammillatus, the club urchin, is highly prized for reef tanks. It is often called the slate-pencil urchin as the spines can be used to write on slate, nearly as well as chalk. Photo by Alan Power.

(L): Long-spined sea urchins, like this *Diadema antillarum*, should be handled with care as the spines are painful if you get stuck. Photo by P. Colin.

(R): *Echinometra viridis* lives in holes and crevices in the reef. The dark tips to the spines aid in its identification. Photo by P. Colin.

The spines of the club-spined sea urchins (species of the genus *Heterocentrotus*) are often used to make wind chimes. This specimen came from the Maldive Islands. Photo by Dr. Herbert R. Axelrod.

rolling right over an anemone, damaging it badly.

Sea Apple (*Pseudocolochirus axiologus*)

The sea apple is a filter-feeding sea cucumber that is very popular in the reef aquarium. Certainly, the species has much to recommend it. There is nothing more alien in appearance or action. It uses the feathery arms to comb the water for plankton, and each arm is pushed to the "mouth" in turn, constantly feeding the

Sea apples, like this *Pseudocolochirus tricolor*, are very colorful sea cucumbers. They use their feathery arms to collect plankton, and each arm alternately brings the food into the mouth. Photo by M. P. and C. Piednoir.

animal. In their natural habitat in the Indo-Pacific, they will feed primarily at night when the plankton is out and many of the predators are not. However, in the home aquarium they will often feed during the day. Part of the reason for this is that they are, unfortunately, starving. The reef tanker must be very diligent about frequent feedings (at least once a day) of a suitable substitute plankton food, consisting of specially formulated liquid foods and of newly-hatched brine shrimp. Properly tended to, these sea cucumbers can be the main attraction in a reef tank.

Feather Cucumber (*Cucumaria miniata*)

This small and feathery sea cucumber from the Indo-Pacific is relatively hardy, but it must be fed much like the sea apple. There are several color varieties of this species. One of the most attractive has bright yellow feathery tentacles and tube feet down the sides of the body, which itself is of a pinkish hue. One of the bad things about these species of sea cucumber is that you must exclude fishes that may pick at them—and that includes an awful lot of fishes! One of the good things is that if you keep several specimens, they may reproduce in the aquarium. If such a thing happens, you may find clusters of miniature adults adhering to the rocks, coral, and sides of the tank.

One of the feather sea cucumbers, *Cucumaria insolens* from South Africa. Fishes or other animals that are attracted to the feathery arms and that might nibble on them should be excluded from the aquarium. Photo by T. E. Thompson.

Cucumaria miniata is widely spread over the Indo-Pacific. This individual is from California. These small cucumbers when kept in small groups may even reproduce in the reef aquarium. Photo by D. Gotshall.

One of the joys of setting up a mini-reef is to go out and collect your own oddities. At the same time you can become aware of their living habits and know what they need to keep them happy. Photo of Evelyn Axelrod by Dr. Herbert R. Axelrod.

FISHES FOR THE REEF TANK

There are several approaches to including fishes in a reef tank. The most radical is not to include any fishes at all. Some reef keepers are avid adherents to this school. Their interest in reef animals has progressed to the point that they don't want to endanger the invertebrates in their tank, and they can live without the fishes. Most of us would balk at such a stark approach. Fishes provide movement and contrasting color which help give the reef tank the beauty for which it is justifiably famous.

Another approach is to have different fish species in the tank at different stages of development of the tank. For example, when the living rock is in place and has reached a reasonably stable stage, a hobbyist may place a fish in it that will hunt down any mantis shrimp which may be in the tank. Candidates for this job would be a triggerfish, such as the Picasso trigger (*Rhinecanthus aculeatus*), or tilefishes, such as the flashing tilefish (*Hoplolatilus chlupatyi*). A hobbyist places such a fish in the tank with the knowledge that the fish will most assuredly damage any desirable shrimp, too—but somehow the desirable ones aren't usually "smuggled"

A candidate for the job of hunting down an unwanted mantis shrimp in a reef tank would be the Picasso triggerfish, *Rhinecanthus aculeatus*. Photo by M. P. and C. Piednoir.

Fishes with long snouts, like this *Chelmon rostratus*, are able to pick food out from cracks and crevices and other less accessible places. Photo by M. P. and C. Piednoir.

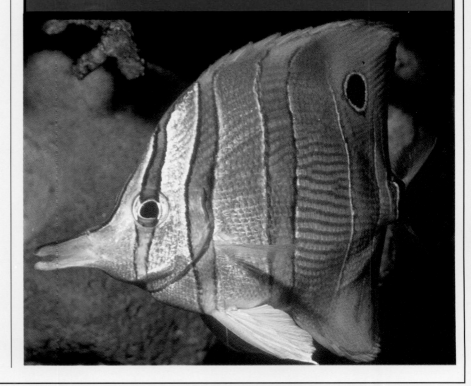

in with the live rock! Another worry about this approach is that the triggerfish, in particular, is going to browse on desirable growths on the live rock, too, such as tube worms and any corals that may have colonized the live rock. Another drawback to this approach is that the fishes must eventually be removed from the tank before the coral, anemones, and other inhabitants are placed inside. It is almost always necessary to completely dismantle a tank to take out a fish, and reef tankers aren't as casual about doing such a thing—even with only live rock in the tank—as your normal aquarist. Still, the value of putting in these "mop up" fishes during the latter part of the live rock acclimation is sufficient that a number of hobbyists do it. Whether you do it or not, you have to then consider what fishes to put in the final version of your reef tank. Some tilefishes can be left in the tank as long as you aren't keeping any crabs or shrimps.

Another pest that can come in with live rock are the so-called glass anemones. These are disgustingly fecund and can cause lots of problems in a reef tank. When they occur, most hobbyists resign themselves to having to remove them periodically by picking them off with tweezers or forceps and scraping them off flat surfaces with a razor blade. Now is the time to get rid of all of them by introducing a butterflyfish, such as the

copperband butterflyfish, *Chelmon rostratus.* You might even be able to leave this fish in the tank as long as you don't keep any fan or Christmas tree worms.

The most common approach is to select fishes that will co-exist well with the invertebrate inhabitants of a reef tank. There are two main problems in keeping fishes with invertebrates. The first is that fishes have a tendency to feed upon invertebrates.

Gramma loreto is one of the big favorites for reef tanks, but it is difficult to keep more than one in a tank. Photo by Cathy Church.

In the wild this characteristic is not a problem, for the number of fishes is automatically adjusted so that they are much less numerous than the invertebrates. Any time a fish population is sufficient that it diminishes a prey item, such as anemones or corals, the

fish population is diminished, too, so that there is a homeostatic relationship of the type that exists between all predators and their prey. In any case, in the ocean, fishes are like insects buzzing around in a forest, so vast is the reserve of corals and other invertebrates. In even the most abundant reef tank, the balance has been tipped in the other direction by a considerable margin.

So what we want are fishes that are not inclined to eat the invertebrates— most especially the corals. But a further problem with fishes is that their greater metabolic rate has a tendency to raise havoc with the near-perfect water quality that we must maintain for a reef tank. One thing that hobbyists like to do is to include fishes that can be fed only three times a week. That sounds good, but such fishes (usually basslets) must be fed good sized meals. Is the final effect any worse than maintaining fishes that eat just a tiny amount daily? I'm inclined to doubt that it is, as we are dealing with a given volume of waste. Just the fact that it is not evacuated as often should not mislead us into thinking that it is less.

Hobbyists like fishes that can be fed the same food that the invertebrates eat, such as plankton or newly-hatched brine shrimp. The only catch to that is that the fishes need to be fed more often than the invertebrates (which have

The flashing tilefish, *Hoplolatilus chlupatyi*, is capable of removing mantis shrimp (and other crustaceans) from your tank. Photo by Ken Lucas.

Gramma loreto is primarily a plankton feeding fish that will accept brine shrimp as a reasonable substitute. It should be fed every day if possible. Photo by Cathy Church.

All species of lionfishes *(Pterois)* are potentally dangerous. Be very careful when handling them. Photo by M.P. & C. Piednoir.

supplemental nutrition from their photosynthetic zooxanthellae). Another possible problem is that a lot of the fishes that feed on planktonic resources also have a tendency to browse around on the tank's invertebrates. Some of the clownfishes are surprisingly culpable here. The ideal species will feed primarily on algae, thus ridding the aquarium of this bane of most reef keeper's existence, and, thus, endearing itself all the more to him or her.

In any case, the following species are selected with the idea in mind that, first, they will do no harm. If they can be helpful in some way, so much the better. But it should be emphasized that including fishes is a complication, and that is the very reason that a number of reef keepers have decided to do without them. Such an approach has been likened to having a garden without the butterflies and birds, and most hobbyists are going to want to keep at least some of the fish species.

No attempt has been made to list the fishes here in any phylogenetic order. Rather, the fishes listed first are the ones that are most compatible with the organisms in a reef tank and contribute best to it, both in regard to appearance and in other ways.

ROYAL GRAMMA (*GRAMMA LORETO*)

This little jewel from the Caribbean, looking for all

the world as though it had been dipped in Easter egg dye, is surely in the running for the title of the most beautiful fish in the world. They are seen in bunches in coral areas, but each has its own hole or cave in which it usually resides upside down. Although they seem to congregate together in the wild, it is extremely difficult to keep more than one in an aquarium. They are primarily plankton feeders in the wild, and they will take newly-hatched brine shrimp and thrive on it even as adults. Although this little beauty is

extremely aggressive with others of its species, it is generally peaceful with other fishes. The main drawback with this gem is that it should be fed daily; however, it can subsist on feedings of newly-hatched brine shrimp and liquid plankton food that are given four times a week. Watch it carefully during this time, though, to be sure that it is thriving.

FLASHER WRASSES (*PARACHEILINUS* SPECIES)

Wrasses are normally the last fishes we would want in a reef tank, as wrasses are equipped with effective

Paracheilinus octotaenia is one of the flasher wrasses. They apparently got this name from the habit of males displaying and lighting up in color when they encounter each other. Photo by Helmut Debelius.

teeth for decimating invertebrates, and many species specialize in feeding upon them. However, the flasher wrasses are small in size, rarely exceeding three inches, and they don't bother invertebrates. They feed upon plankton and come from the Indian Ocean and South Pacific. Members of this group are known for their strange double pupil, an adaptation that is assumed to aid in locating small prey items.

Paracheilinus species occur in aggregates that rise in the water column, turn into the current, and feed upon the plankton that the current brings them. Many wrasses live in harems and are protogynous hermaphrodites, meaning that they can change sex from female to male. It is possible to keep a group of these very pretty fish in a reef tank. The best way to do this may be to mix the

The flasher wrasses, including this *Paracheilinus carpenteri,* are peaceful with other species but males of the same species will fight prolonged battles. Photo by Aaron Norman.

species, as males from the same species will fight prolonged battles. Some of the species available in this country are *Paracheilinus octotaenia, P. filamentosus, P. carpenteri, P. mccoskeri, P. angulatus,* and *P. lineopunctatus.*

The flasher wrasses help add color and movement to the reef tank, and they are peaceful with other species; in fact, their tank mates must be picked carefully, as they can be bullied by more aggressive fishes. If they are to be housed with fiery damselfishes (e.g. any damselfish!), they should be introduced first and

allowed to have a week, at the very least, to establish themselves in the tank. They get their name "flasher wrasses" from the habit of males displaying and lighting up in color when they encounter each other.

CHECKER FAIRY BASSLET (*PSEUDANTHIAS PLEUROTAENIA*)

If this species is kept, you will want to forego the flasher wrasses, as these have a similar life style and appearance. They apparently recognize each other as competitors for the

Paracheilinus filamentosus, like other members of the genus, are plankton feeders that rise up in the water column and pick out food items that the current brings them. Photo by Dr. G. R. Allen.

The checker fairy basslet, *Pseudanthias pleurotaenia*, may regard the flasher wrasses as rivals for the same food and attack them. It is best not to keep these fishes together. Photo by R. Sprackland.

Fairy basslets are gregarious fishes that are best kept in groups. Perhaps one male and several females would be the correct way to go. *Pseudanthias hutchi* in the Solomon Islands. Photo by Dr. G. R. Allen.

One of the less common species of fairy basslet is this *Pseudanthias fasciatus*. Nevertheless its care is the same as the other members of the genus. Photo by Aaron Norman.

plankton, and the fairy basslets attack the flashers relentlessly. The care of this species is very similar to the foregoing ones. This particular species hails from the Red Sea, but many species are found all over the South Pacific and Indian Ocean. Other similar species that are suitable for the reef tank are *Pseudanthias hutchi, P. fasciatus, P. taeniatus,* and *P. pictilis,* to name just a few. These species are just a little larger than the flasher wrasses, generally reaching about four inches maximum length.

In view of the superficial similarity between the flasher wrasses and the fairy basslets, the decision on which to keep may depend on the availability of species, as well as personal taste.

Pseudanthias taeniatus comes from the Red Sea. Therefore, it will probably do better in the higher temperature range. Photo by Helmut Debelius.

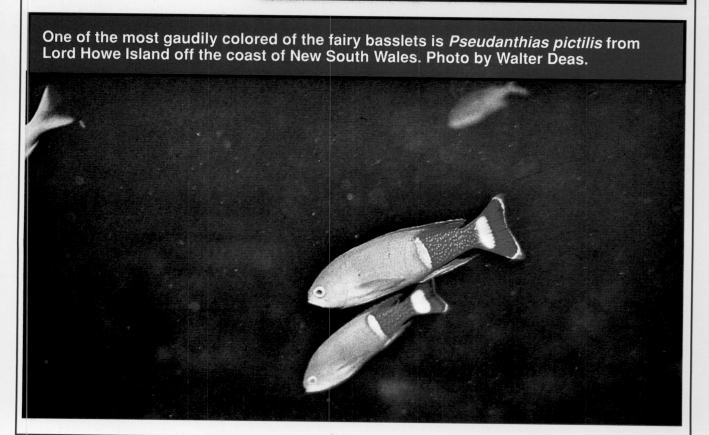

One of the most gaudily colored of the fairy basslets is *Pseudanthias pictilis* from Lord Howe Island off the coast of New South Wales. Photo by Walter Deas.

SEAHORSES (*HIPPOCAMPUS* SPECIES)

Although there is no worry about the seahorses bothering the coral or eating any of your shrimp or crabs, there are a couple of problems with keeping these very emblems of the sea. First, there must be nearly a constant supply of food in the tank. That works against our goal to keep the water super clean. A good food is newly-hatched brine shrimp, and they will survive in the reef tank for a long time; however, they will be sucked in by your filters and protein skimmers. One of the prices we pay for keeping these very unique fishes in a reef tank is that we must constantly change the prefilters for any filtration devices and protein skimmers.

Another problem is that the tank mates for the seahorses must be selected with care. In nature, seahorses cling to eel grass, sargassum weed, or fan corals by their prehensile tails and feed upon the plankton that the current brings them. Active fishes are likely to out compete them for food or harass them so that they don't eat properly. I have seen them prosper in tanks with flasher wrasses and with mandarin fishes. If you have anemones in your tank, you would want to pass up seahorses, as they don't seem to recognize the anemones as being dangerous, as do most other fishes, and will make no effort to stay away from them.

Sea horses must have some slender objects that they can cling to with their prehensile tails. This is *Hippocampus reidi* from Grand Cayman, B. W. I. Photo by Cathy Church.

DOTTYBACKS (*PSEUDOCHROMIS* SPECIES)

These species are sometimes referred to as dwarf groupers. A good example is the neon-striped basslet, *Pseudochromis dutoiti*. Very few of these species get to be more than four inches in length. These are some of the most suitable fishes for

A good food for *Hippocampus* species is newly hatched brine shrimp, but the food must be almost constantly available for them. They also do not recognize sea anemones as potentially dangerous. Photo by M. P. and C. Piednoir.

Hippocampus erectus is probably the most common sea horse available. It comes from the western Atlantic and may appear in a variety of colors. Photo by J. Kelly Giwojna.

the invertebrate tank, as they are quite colorful, with iridescent combinations of red, purple, yellow, orange, blue, gold, and black. Fishes of the same species are territorial toward each other, so don't try to keep an aggregate of these fishes. Rather keep quite differently-colored fishes of different species. Most of these species will eat bits of clam and dry food; however, some may dine on small shrimps, but they won't bother corals or anemones.

LONG-NOSED BUTTERFLYFISH (*FORCIPIGER LONGIROSTRIS*)

Funny how some species can look delicate and actually be quite hardy and vice versa. The long-nosed butterflyfish is an example

Keeping an aggregate of these orchid dottybacks, *Pseudochromis fridmani*, may be a mistake as they tend to be territorial. Photo by Gunter Spies.

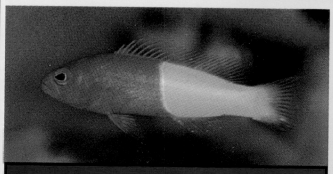

Pseudochromis paccagnellae is a favorite of reef tank keepers because of its bright magenta and gold coloration. Photo by Dr. Herbert R. Axelrod.

The Aldabra dottyback, *Pseudochromis aldabraensis*, is often mistaken for its almost look-alike P. dutoiti. The easiest way to distinguish them is by the tail fin pattern. Photo by Roger Lubbock.

Blue-striped dottyback, *Pseudochromis cyanotaenia*. These mini-groupers will eat bits of clam and dry food. They may eat some of your small shrimps, but do not bother corals or anemones. Photo by Aaron Norman.

The pyramid butterflyfish, *Hemitaurichthys polylepis*, is a good candidate for the reef tank. It will not harm corals or other sessile invertebrates, but it does get fairly large for a reef tank. Photo by M. P. and C. Piednoir.

Forcipiger longirostris may help rid the tank of infestations of tiny bristleworms and glass anemones. It will also pick algae and tiny crustaceans from deep inside the coral and rock with its long snout. Photo by M. P. and C. Piednoir.

of a species that looks delicate and certainly looks like a specialized feeder, what with its long snout and all. But the fact is that this species is quite hardy, and it will pick algae and tiny crustaceans from inside the coral and live rock. It may even help control infestations of tiny bristle worms and glass anemones. Another butterflyfish that is a good candidate for the reef tank is the pyramid butterflyfish, *Hemitaurichthys polylepis*. Both of these species add color and won't harm the corals or other sessile invertebrates. The only thing to keep in mind is that they can each attain about seven inches in length.

SOARING HAWKFISH (*CYPRINOCIRRHITES POLYACTUS*)

Hawkfishes are named for their propensity to perch upon a high rock or coral and "swoop" down upon prey. They are highly prized for reef tanks, as they are hardy. However, most species will eat shrimp and small crabs. This one is generally considered safe with shrimp, crabs, and even small fishes. The only problem it might cause is that hawkfishes sometimes find a favorite place to perch. If this spot happens to be on a valued coral, the mere physical and continuous presence of the fish may injure and even kill the corals in the vicinity.

YELLOW-HEADED JAWFISH (*OPISTOGNATHUS AURIFRONS*)

Jawfishes dig a little vertical cave in which they like to dwell. They even decorate the entrance with rocks. Apparently, this is a type of status symbol. This species is full of personality, as all the jawfishes are, and it only reaches about four inches in length. It most assuredly will not harm the corals and is only a very remote danger to small shrimp.

FORK-TAILED BLENNY (*MEIACANTHUS OVALANENSIS*)

These pretty little fish only get to be about three inches long, and they do beautifully in a reef tank, harming neither the corals nor the shrimp and crabs. They are hardy and feed well, eventually learning to take even dry foods. Again, this is a fish that should be fed on a daily basis, but that may be their only drawback for a reef tank. And a couple of good protein skimmers (or even one big one) will take care of that very minor fault.

BLUE DAMSEL (*CHRYSIPTERA CYANEA*)

This species is sometimes referred to as the "blue devil," but it is actually less aggressive than most of the other damsels. One reason for that is that it tends to school and doesn't hold a clearly defined territory as is the case with so many infamous damsels. There are several color varieties of this single species, as they

Soaring hawkfish, *Cyprinocirrhites polyactis*. Hawkfishes like to perch on a high rock or piece of coral and "swoop" down on their prey, hence the common name. Photo by Dr. D. Terver, Nancy Aquarium.

The yellow-headed jawfish, *Opistognathus aurifrons*, dig a burrow, the edge of which is usually decorated with small stones. It is a mouthbrooder, with the individual seen here holding a mouthful of eggs. Photo by Cathy Church.

Sphaeramia nematoptera is one of the few cardinalfishes that stay out during the day. Photo by M.P. & C. Piednoir.

The fork-tailed blenny, *Meiacanthus oualanensis*, is hardy and eats well, harming neither shrimp nor crabs. They also only grow to three inches in length. Photo by Dr. G. R. Allen.

One of the more common fishes available to marine aquarists is the blue damsel or blue devil, *Chrysiptera cyanea*. It is actually less aggressive than most of the other damsels despite the common name. Photo by Burkhard Kahl.

vary from one location to another in which they are found in the South Pacific, with some species sporting yellow tails. There are other damsels for the reef aquarium that are not a danger to the crustaceans, fishes, or corals, and one of the most beautiful is the canary damsel, *Chrysiptera galba*. The damsels, members of the family Pomacentridae, are generally characterized by extremely aggressive behavior toward fishes and invertebrates, as they tend to hold territories in the wild, driving off all comers. And, of course, their "targets" don't have any place to go in the aquarium.

MAROON CLOWNFISH (*PREMNAS BIACULEATUS*)

The clownfishes are also members of the Pomacentridae and, although they are not quite as hardy and not quite as aggressive as other members of the family, they are more aggressive than members of the genus *Chrysiptera*. In a reef tank, they can cause problems by picking at tubeworms and anemones. If they have their own anemone and are kept well fed, this species is one of the best bets of the anemonefishes (or clownfishes), as they are hardy, and you can keep just one pair of them in the tank. Without an anemone, I wouldn't recommend a clownfish for a reef tank—in spite of all their beauty! However, you may want to think about them for a tank of anemones with clownfishes and no other invertebrates.

THE FIREFISH (*NEMATELEOTRIS DECORA*)

This species feeds upon newly-hatched brine shrimp, and it can be trusted not to harm corals, anemones, shrimp and crabs. Add to this the exotic appearance and hardiness of the species, and we have a real winning combination. It only reaches a maximum size of about three inches, so it 'measures up" (or down!) in the size category, too. These fish get along well, so it is possible to keep a school of these beautiful little fish. It is also possible to combine them with any of the fishes listed above. A true asset to the reef tank!

YELLOW TANG (*ZEBRASOMA FLAVESCENS*)

An important point to remember is that many of the tangs are yellow in their juvenile stage only. To add to the confusion, they are still called "yellow tangs." It is important to ask if the species is imported from Hawaii. That way you can be reasonably certain at getting the proper species. One of the important things about the true yellow tang is that it stays yellow when mature. This may be a moot point, as even the true yellow tang eventually gets too large for most reef tanks, achieving about eight inches in length. The good part is that it takes it about three years to reach that size. Another good thing about yellow tangs is

One of the prettiest damsels is the canary damsel, *Chrysiptera galba*. It is a relatively safe addition to a reef tank and will add some movement and color. Photo by dr. John E. Randall.

The scientific species name of *Premnas biaculeatus* means two-spined, referring to the pair of spines present below the eye. Photo by Dr. Herbert R. Axelrod.

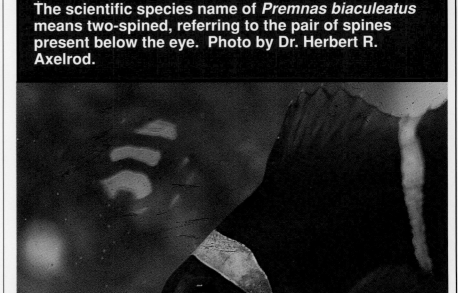

The maroon clownfish, *Premnas biaculeatus*, if provided with their own anemone and sufficient food, will do well in a reef tank. If not well fed they may cause problems by picking at tube worms and anemones. Photo by Burkhard Kahl.

The decorated firefish, *Nemateleotris decora*, is a true asset to a reef tank. It is hardy, beautiful, small, and can be trusted with corals, anemones, and most crustaceans. Photo by Dr. G. R. Allen.

that they eat all types of algae.

The yellow tang is sometimes referred to as the canary of coral fishes, as it will be the first one to let you know when your water conditions are not up to par. It will show signs of distress, such as rapid breathing and huddling in a corner of the tank, and, if the conditions aren't corrected it will die. As demanding as it is of water quality, it has more tolerance for bad water than most of the invertebrate reef denizens, so if your yellow tang is in distress, the other organisms will soon follow. For that reason (as well as to save the yellow tang), it behooves the reef tanker to immediately check the water parameters and make the necessary changes. (A first step would be to make partial changes of water. Then check on the protein skimmer and any filters you have operating.)

The tangs are generally peaceful fishes, but they have a deadly retractable blade at the base of their tail. For that reason, they are sometimes referred to as surgeonfishes, as the tiny "scalpel" is certainly capable of doing some "surgery" on other tank inhabitants. Fortunately, the weapon is almost completely defensive. In my experience, the only time it is used offensively is against other tangs. This species is one of those that occurs in schools in nature but must usually be kept alone in the aquarium. The only exception is in extremely large tanks in which several specimens can be kept together.

The firefish, Nemateleotris magnifica, does well in groups. It is a plankton feeder that does well on newly hatched brine shrimp. Photo by M. P. and C. Piednoir.

The yellow tang, *Zebrasoma flavescens*, will be one of the first animals to let you know that your water conditions are not up to par. For that reason it is sometimes known as the canary of coral fishes. Photo by Will Mara.

INDEX

SUGGESTED READING

H-1101
Hard Cover, 5 ½ x 8 ½", 416
pages. Over 300 color photos.

H-971
Hard Cover, 5 ½ x 8 ½",
512 pages. 432 color photos.

PS-658
Hard Cover, 5 ½ x 8", 240
pages. 119 color photos.

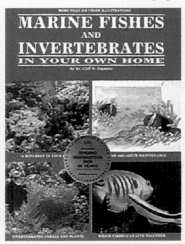

H-1103
Hard Cover, 8 ½ x 11", 192 pages,
315 color photos.

TS-133
Hard Cover, 8 ½ x 11".

TT-027
Hard Cover, 7 x 10", 320
pages. Over 150 color photos.

H-951
Hard Cover, 5 ½ x 8", 736
pages. 600 color photos.